I JUST WANT TO MATTER

ISBN-13: 978-0-57867473-5
ISBN-10-0578674735

Scriptures taken from the HOLY BIBLE, NEW INTERNATIONAL VERSION®. NIV®. Copyright © 1973, 1978, 1984 by International Bible Society. Used by permission of Zondervan. All rights reserved worldwide.

Scripture quotations marked MSG are taken from *THE*

MESSAGE   , copyright © 1993, 1994, 1995, 1996, 2000, 2001,

2002 by Eugene H.

Peterson. Used by permission of NavPress. All rights reserved. Represented by Tyndale House Publishers, Inc.

Cover and Interior Design by: *Designed by Evelyn*

Editorial services by: *Yolanda Harris*

Editorial, proofing, fact-checking, and publishing services provided by:
Carmen The Wordsmith Hope Christmas-Gaude,
CarsamontePublishing@gmail.com.

DEDICATION

I dedicate this book to my loving husband, Ed Cheltenham. Thank you for the tremendous patience, concern and support you have shown in each of my endeavors for the last 44 years of our marriage. I love you more each day!

ACKNOWLEDGEMENTS

It is with heart-felt thanks that I acknowledge Renita Clayton who pumped and prodded me to continue this work to completion. Your encouragement sustained me from beginning to end.

Special thanks to my partners in ministry. Your prayers and endless support provide the strength on which I humbly stand.

I also want to acknowledge Yolanda Harris: editor extraordinaire! You have been my encourager, my voice, my pen and my polisher. Thank you for reminding me of the vision God has given me as an author. You have been there for me in ways that I could never fully explain. Thanks for never letting me down. I must acknowledge Carmen Glover the Wordsmith for her skills, abilities, guidance, and her gift of encouragement. It is by her hands that I was able to bring this gift forward, thank you for excellent, compassionate service in helping me birth, proof and publish this baby.

Finally, to all those who will read this book. May you come to understand that in the full scheme of things, you truly matter. Maintaining an "I matter" mindset is the optimum stance in life! It is not wealth, power nor standing on a grand stage that will propel you forward in life. Rather, it is knowing your value in Christ that will ignite the doors of destiny to swing open on your behalf! After reading this book it is my desire that you find great comfort in knowing that when you take your final breath, it will be just like inhaling sweet air, knowing that you mattered to at least One!

CONTENTS

INTRODUCTION

When we were growing up, each of us aspired to pursue a certain path or career. Some had great plans to attend college and pursue advanced degrees so that we could make big bucks as a top- ranking executive in a Fortune 500 Company. There were also those who planned to move to some adventurous city like Hollywood, New York, or Los Angeles to become famous. Others decided they would use their talents to launch their own businesses. Still others desired a simple life, with a safe home, well-mannered children, a supportive family, and great friends. The list of possibilities of what a girl could or would be can go on for miles!

You may have been able to find your childhood intentions among the examples listed, or you may have wanted a totally different path that would bring your life-long fulfillment. Whatever the case, ultimately life began to unfold, at times in unpredictable, disappointing, or hurtful ways. Some of us had children, found creative ways to overcome life's setbacks and secured jobs to make ends' meet. Life has a way of surprising us, and we are not always sure how to respond.

If I can speak truthfully, there are moments when we have arrived at a certain juncture in life and wondered, *How did I get here?* In retrospect, we think of the aspirations we had when we were younger. We had a plan, there was no room for fear, and we were unstoppable! But along the way, we either put our dreams on hold, someone convinced us we were not good enough or perhaps we stopped dreaming altogether. After we have endured trials and tests, we become weary, we lose confidence, and sometimes feel guilty. I'm not suggesting none of our dreams ever come true, nor am I suggesting they never will. I've just lived long enough to know that each of us, at times, have been hindered by events that were out of our control. We may have even suffered low self-esteem, poor decisions or a lack of focus and direction. I've also lived long enough to know that God's plans for us are still beyond anything that we can think or imagine. He can use everything we have gone through to uncover the diamond within us all!

Having met, ministered, and counseled with countless women over the years, I have found some common threads that most of us share. In this book, I reveal a few. As you read, I want to encourage you to reclaim your life, your joy, and your dreams. Be confident for there truly is a queen on the inside just bursting to get out! I believe that no matter how difficult the journey, or how hopeless the nights may seem at times, we each have within us everything we need to get back up again and soar! It is not too late. Believe that!

You may be at a great place in your life, and I celebrate you for that. But I want to encourage you to go further. While you may be hugely successful in some areas of your life, maybe you are at a standstill in others. Complete the circle. Find the will and the tenacity to go after whatever it is you desire. Whether you seek a better relationship with someone, greater confidence, or want to take a dream vacation or purchase a home, it is all available to you. Regardless of your current state, ask yourself, *"Am I in the will of God?"* Do my dreams align with

His plan? Have I been

so busy doing what I wanted that I never really considered what He wanted? Have I stopped dreaming, stopped living, stopped believing? Am I only existing? Do I even matter?"

If you can identify with just one of these questions, this book is for you! You are about to change your outlook on life and move closer to your divine destiny. You have a place in God's master plan. He created you intentionally. Regardless of how you feel or what others say or think about you, you matter.

I encourage you to find a journal or notebook to record some of the helpful tools outlined in this book. There are plenty of opportunities for self-reflection, and I'll bet that you will learn new things about yourself that just may surprise you. So, buckle your seatbelt, inhale and exhale, and let's begin this journey together!

CHAPTER ONE
Discovering What *Really* Matters

Every day of our lives, we are bombarded with multiple messages strategically designed to influence the way we think and live. Each one stems from a different source which may include family, social media, the Internet, traditional media, movies, or even the music we enjoy. While some communications are blatant, others are subliminal. Yet, they impact us just the same.

In today's society, it is difficult to pinpoint what is important. The sweeping opinions openly expressed through social media, entertainment headlines and the celebrated voices of our time can be fickle, to say the least. One day, people affiliate themselves with a certain person or group, but the slightest slip up can occur, and they completely abandon ship! The same is true of the latest fashion trend, diet solution or technological discovery. People jump on the bandwagon, and a few months down the line, they are in search of the next *new* thing! The truth of the matter is there are so many ideas coming toward us that it is becoming harder and harder to know what matters, and what does not. If we're not careful, we can easily become conflicted within ourselves without even knowing it.

Take a moment to think about this: What really matters to YOU? What do you consider important, valuable or a priority? Deciding what matters invites us on a journey through the vast ocean of our minds. This journey forces first, the discovery of who we are, our intended purpose, and that which we value most. It can be exhausting to push past all the distractions in life such as people, work, relationships, disappointment, and pain. At times, the journey may force us to dig through periods of our past that

---

"At the end of life, what really matters is not what we bought but what we built; not what we got but what we shared; not our competence but out character; and not our success, but our significance. Live a life that matters. Live a life of love...."
AUTHOR

UNKNOWN

---

may be associated with traumatic events or counterproductive habits that endangered our well-being in some way. It is in these difficult areas of our lives that we uncover unfulfilled promises, abandoned dreams and painful memories. Unfortunately, the baggage we carry oftentimes becomes the very thing that hinders us from living our best lives. However, to move from where we are today to where we ultimately desire to be, overcoming life's distractions and deciding what really matters is a necessary step.

THRIVING AFTER A SETBACK

What we believe is intricately tied to the way we act. If our belief system and therefore our behaviors are tied to outward distractions, we never have to own our decisions or monitor what we do. Sure, it matters that a person has lived through difficult times. However, it is equally important that the person not allow the experience to hinder his or her progress. This is the ultimate test. Most people have been in that place at one time or another. Maybe you were outgoing, successful and confident, but after going through a tough situation, you somehow lost your zeal. Whatever you have gone through, no matter how painful or unfair, it is not the end-all! Perhaps you lost a loved one, your home or job, served time in prison, or were violated in some way. God can heal your broken heart. In fact, He promises that He will. Psalm 147: 3 says, "He heals the brokenhearted and binds up their wounds." (*NIV*) Not only will God heal you; He will remove the evidence of its impact on your life.

Regardless of our struggles, we must utilize our faith to overcome life's obstacles. It is one thing for the people around us to have faith for us, but it is yet another for us to believe that *our* faith can move mountains. Sometimes we allow our circumstances to define who we are, but this way of thinking limits our ability to thrive. Ultimately, each of us must determine within ourselves; what God has promised us is worth the fight.

Life's setbacks provide us with an array of predetermined demands that can potentially hold our thoughts and desires captive. Circumstances also influence the way we view ourselves and our potential for success. For example, a person who has been in an abusive relationship may see themselves as unworthy of anything better. They were devalued for so long that they themselves begin to buy into the lie. Not always immediately, but over the course of time with the falling and getting back up again, a person can simply lose sight of who they really are.

By the same token, a person who has less education than his or her counterparts may feel unqualified to seek promotion for a higher paying position. Feelings of inadequacy and inferiority can become embedded in a person's mind, causing them to lose confidence. Societal norms often contribute to these beliefs when in reality the individual not only possesses the potential to do and become more, they have the God-given right to do so!

It is for these reasons and countless others that we must continually reevaluate that which is important to us, independent of what others think or believe. In doing so, we clear the clutter in our minds so that we may confidently pursue that which we seek with greater clarity. There exists within each of us, a predestined purpose and passion ready to unfold. This spiritual awakening can occur at any time. In fact, you may have already tapped into it – in part. However, to maximize your potential, you must dig deeply into the depths of your heart for hidden clues that can only be found within the city of your soul. Difficult times tend to push us toward finding meaning in our lives, thereby strengthening our relationship with the Creator.

PROTECT YOUR TREASURE

We were not designed to be a cheap imitation of someone else, or a copycat of some fantasy. Playing these roles puts us in a position of vulnerability. Before we know it, we have fallen victim to seeking approval from an audience or individual that will never be fully satisfied. When we compare ourselves to others, we will never measure up. Instead, we will come up short every single time. The hardest part is trying to maintain the facade. It can be frustrating! By attempting to please others, we ultimately live for their applause. In essence, we perform for an audience that loves the lie rather than the truth of who we *really* are. Until we are true to ourselves, we cannot win!

Unveiling your personal truth can only be achieved by permission. You must give yourself permission to see and accept yourself just as you are – gifts, thoughts, flaws, past, present and everything in between. The intention is not to be self-critical, rather self-knowing.

Knowing who you really are – the person God intended you to be – will open your eyes to understanding *why* you matter. The soul-searching required to achieve this goal must be an intentional effort toward personal intimacy. When you look at this word closely and say it phonetically, it becomes clearer: *in-to-me- see!* Intimacy allows you to peel back the onion so-to-speak. Just as with onions, this process may also produce a few tears. However, once you tap into the revelation of what truly matters, you will find it necessary to protect this new-found treasure.

The gift of intimacy can only be afforded to those who enter a genuine relationship with you, and rightly so! The time, patience and discernment needed to see who you really are can only be shared with those who deserve it. The real you cannot be realized in a momentary glimpse. Passersby need to keep on stepping! Why? Not everyone is worthy or trustworthy enough to be in relationship with you. When you allow yourself to be completely open to just anyone, you are left in the rubble of your own hurt, frustration, and brokenness.

SEEKING PURPOSE

The danger of relying on what someone else wants or believes about you, will send you spiraling down a rabbit hole. In other words, you will enter a situation that can easily become problematic as it unfolds. When life becomes chaotic, we find ourselves asking age-old questions like *"Who am I?" "Why was I born?" "Do I really matter?"* These questions will torment your very existence, until you take the time to answer them. Each of us will arrive at this place at least once in our lifetime. Some revisit this place several times throughout their lifetime.

These questions cannot be ignored. They are like the giant, Goliath, that David faced: Relentless, intimidating, and unyielding. Yet, the key to discovering your purpose can be revealed in the answers to these questions. When you know your purpose, you understand why you matter. This realization is an invitation to step onto the floor of life and dance to the music of your very own choices.

We have each been given the gift of choice, or free-will. Many may see this gift as a curse because their choices have led to a mediocre and mundane existence. The power to choose empowers us to move any mountain, or challenge, we may face. Though our circumstance or concerns may be as tall as Mt. Everest, it can and will move when we apply faith. *"Truly I tell you, if anyone says to this mountain, 'Go, throw yourself into the sea,' and does not doubt in their heart but believes that what they say will happen, it will be done for them."* (Mark 11:23, *NIV*)

THE JOURNEY BEGINS

The journey toward understanding why you matter is a positive step in the right direction. It will be uncomfortable at times but keep going. You will travel through the good, the bad and the ugly thoughts, experiences, fears and frustrations you have gone through over the years. The journey will bring up old memories including some that have had a negative impact on your progress.

Many people are tormented by childhood memories that continue to replay in their adult dreams. Some are reminded of an uninvited touch or the groping of someone who stole their innocence. As a result, the budding flower of hope of the little girl who was intended to become a queen or the little boy who was intended to become a king was diminished. For others, the memory of the untimely death of a parent, grandparent or sibling is like an open wound. Then there are those who lived through their childhood with the absence of a parent who left them behind or was preoccupied with other things that distracted him or her from playing a vital role in their lives.

Whether the difficulties you have endured have been few or endless, they expose potholes and pit stops along life's journey that seek to define or devalue your worth. Over time, they become weights that delay you from reaching your destiny. The hills and valleys of failed relationships, businesses and the pursuit of dreams attempt to undermine why you matter. The residue of having to walk through the Valley of the Shadow of Death presents itself in every area of your life. Somewhere along the way, you may have reached a plateau, and you just can't seem to move forward. It is like getting to the place in your weight-loss journey where progress just stops. No matter how many healthy foods you eat or how many days you work out, the scale reads the same.

The mind is like a computer. It can work to our advantage or disadvantage. It records and replays the good and the bad. Unfortunately, traumatic, and regretful events tend to be high on the re-run playlist. Each time they play, rest and peace are disturbed. If you're not careful, these thoughts will bully you into accepting the idea that you are a victim rather than a victor.

I once heard someone say something along these lines: "Free your mind and your body will follow." There is some truth to this statement. Like a computer, we often wish we had the ability to permanently delete the unwanted files in our minds. It would certainly free up space for better, lasting, and beneficial memories. Many medical studies have proven that there is a direct correlation between mental and physical health. It is interesting to read how depression and sadness tends to follow physical illness. It is also true that the way we feel about our lives will have a drastic impact on how well our bodies perform over time.

The Bible tells us that as a man thinks in his heart, so is he! In other words, what you think in your mind and believe in your heart is inevitably what you will become. Taking care of your mind and body is God's desire. Scripture says, *"Beloved, I pray that you may prosper in all things and be in health, just as your soul [mind] prospers."* (3 John 2, *NKJV*) God is indicating in this passage that a prosperous mind (soul) is in direct alignment with good health.

Scientists have traced the emotional responses of the brain to the quality and value we place on our lives. When we give into the stressors of life, thereby damaging our belief system, we don't believe that we really matter. The problem with this train of thought is that we fail to measure our worth by the One who created us. That is opposite to God's plan. We must renew our minds through His Word to correct our mindset. I was reading an article in "Life Journal" that addressed the mind, emotion and body connection. It stated, *"In a very simplified way, an emotion starts with an emotional stimulus being received by a sense organ. This information is relayed to the limbic system, which is the brain's very domineering emotional processing area.*

It is located centrally in the brain, connects to most other brain

areas and many body parts and regulates chemicals that affect how

the entire brain operates" (LeDoux, 2002).

"But, my friend, I ask, "Who do you think you are to question God?

Does the clay have the right to ask the potter why he shaped it

the way he did?" (Romans 9:20, *CEV*)

Likely, there have been many occasions when we have questioned about what God had in mind when He created us. Yet, just as likely, people have said things that made us feel inadequate thereby causing us to doubt that God had any plan at all for us. Demonstrating our doubt, we make degrading statements like, *"I'm not pretty enough." "I'm too fat." "I'm way too thin." "My hair is too short." "My skin is too dark." "My skin is too white." "So-and-so is more intelligent than I am."* The list goes on and on. Maybe you have subjected yourself to statements like these.

What if we had a say in the matter and could tell God how we wanted Him to create us? Some of us would literally give Him a list of examples to imitate. I imagine someone might tell God: *I want Halle Berry's face; Beyoncé's body and sex appeal, and Oprah's business savvy.* When we compare ourselves to others and devalue how we were created, we are ultimately telling God that He made a mistake. Think about that for a moment: God made a mistake. Really? God has never, nor will He ever, make a mistake. God is not going to change His mind about how He created us.

Since He orchestrated the plan for our lives long before we were conceived in our mother's womb, He is the only One qualified to have the final say. We are each original works of art created by design. Long before you and I began making choices and certainly before other people made choices that would affect the course of our lives, God knew it all. He knew the stumbles and pitfalls we would encounter, so He built us in such a way that we could take a lickin' and keep on tickin'!

As you take this journey toward discovery, I encourage you to fully embrace God's plan for your life. The Almighty One is ready to usher you into your destiny. He knows your past, present and even your future mistakes. If there is anything separating you from God – thoughts, actions, regret or unforgiveness – settle it today. Simply repent and at that very moment, He will forgive you so that you can begin afresh.

Things happen in life that are beyond our control. At times, we become the victim of someone else's poor choices. God doesn't hold us accountable for their actions. He will deal with him or her directly. If you have experienced hurt or some personal setback that has hindered your progress, surrender it to Him. Cast that burden on Him because He cares. Open your heart and mind to receive the new thing God is about to do in your life. He is a healer. He has great plans and an expected end specifically for you! God created you to add beauty to His garden as only you can. Blossom where you have been planted!

CHAPTER 2

Receive the Gift in You!

"For in him all things were created: things in heaven and on earth, visible and   invisible, whether thrones or powers or rulers or authorities; all things have been created through him and for him." (Colossians 1:16, *NIV*)

God has crafted, carved, and molded each of us uniquely according to His design and with His own hands. He created us for His reasons, purposes, and pleasure. With passionate love and determination, God designed our distinguishing features: How we look, the color and texture of our hair, skin and eyes, our body shape, height, and physical structure. All these characteristics make us genuinely

unique.

God created us in the counsel of His own mind. He needed no one's input or approval on what we should look like or what our distinguishing characteristics should be. He was so meticulous in His thoughts toward us that He planned who our parents would be. They may not have planned our arrival; it may have been a huge surprise! But God had you and I on

His mind. He brought together the correct DNA that would produce the magnificent persons we are today!

It is true that many births are unplanned. Painfully I admit, I am the result of one of them. But I am a firm believer that every child is in God's plan. People make mistakes, God does not. He can take our mess and make it undeniably amazing!

God is timeless. He can see all the events and issues of life at the same time: Past, present and future. Our loving Father takes into account all the issues and hardships that may occur in our lives and equips us to overcome them all! God has a master plan for everything and all things. Nothing and no one exist by accident. God put all things into motion, and they live and have their being in

Him.

No Greater Love

You may wonder why God would do all of this for us: more specifically for you. There are many answers, but John 3:16 explains it this way: *"For God so loved the world that he gave his one and only son, that whoever believes in him shall not perish but have eternal life." (NIV) The Voice*

Bible states it this way: "For God expressed His love for the world in this way: He gave His only Son so that whoever believes in Him will not face everlasting destruction, but will have everlasting life." Here's the point. God didn't send His Son into the world to judge it; instead, He came to rescue a world headed toward certain destruction.

God, in His infinite wisdom, did all of this for you! He wants to continue to do wonderful things through you because He loves you! He yearns to be in fellowship with you. God proves His love time and time again. The greatest demonstration is when He gave humanity His very best: His only and His all – His son, Jesus Christ. God is the full expression of love. The Word of God tells us that He *is* love.

It is the Father's great pleasure to express this love to you, His creation. He has chosen you to be the recipient of His immeasurable, immutable love. You don't have to pay for it or do anything to gain it. Just accept it by receiving His Son, Jesus Christ into your heart. This is what salvation is all about. When you make God the center of your life, everything good and perfect comes to you. Does it mean your life will be perfect or that you will no longer encounter disappointment? No. But when you run up against challenges in life, God will be there guiding you through, holding you, and fighting on your behalf.

Many people struggle to find their place and purpose in life. They take many paths to locate that "sweet spot," but miss the mark because they begin the journey by trying to discover themselves. I have heard many people say they were trying to "find" themselves. Then they set out on a personal journey to find the person they lost. Some try mental exploration through meditation or some other metaphysical means of attempting to find themselves. The belief is that they will find purpose. I'm not judging people or their methods. No one wants to live without purpose. Most of us hope that our lives will impact others in some positive way.

Pursuing God

There are many reasons why people are lost and seeking purpose for their empty hearts. However, regardless of method, it is in our seeking that we ultimately find God. We begin to see Him and our relationship with Him in an entirely new light. If you seek purpose for your life, don't waste time in your journey with empty stops. Begin to pursue the God Who pursues you. He pulls at your heartstrings even now, trying to bring you into His outstretched arms and all-encompassing love.

God is inviting you to begin this journey with Him, so you come to realize how much you matter to Him. It doesn't really matter what others say or think about you. After all is said and done, it only matters what God says and thinks about you. Only His words have the power to change your life! Look to His Word (The Bible), everything you need to become successful in your quest for

purpose is there.

You may already have a relationship with God. If so, go deeper. Maybe you once walked with Him, but life's circumstances and lost hope caused you to turn to people and material things. In fact, you may have found your purpose there. Maybe you've done things you are ashamed of and feel you are unworthy of a relationship with God. There is no guilt, anger, pain or sin too great for Him to turn His back. God never rejects us when we seek Him, so come. Ask God to come into your heart and accept the gift of salvation. Being in relationship with Him is the safest place to be, and it is filled with blessings.

You are now ready to explore and learn from God's basic instruction book; The Bible (aka the Word). In it is the road map to your purpose and evidence that you positively matter! By using this book, you will find how fearfully and wonderfully you were made as a one-of-a-kind designer original. You will also discover that God has a specific purpose for you that only you can complete. As you glean from God's Word, you will find peace that surpasses understanding and love overflowing. You will realize that someone's answer is connected to your purpose. Everything you have dreamed about and searched for, begins

here!

Time to Make That Change

"Let us examine our ways and test them and let us return to the Lord."

(Lamentations 3:40, *NIV*)

Most of the time, we spend our lives trying to change our circumstances or the people around us. We struggle to change our looks by changing the color of our hair with dye or the color of our eyes with contact lenses.

Some have used various types of surgery to change their appearance while forgetting their problems are an internal issue. We are not defined by our problems, what people think, or the labels society gives us. Our lives are so much more than the broken pieces we have come to accept, or the fractured image reflected in the mirror. By changing the way we see ourselves, we alter the way we see others and therefore the world.

Change challenges us to lay down the weight of issues that may have been plaguing our lives for years. Feelings of inadequacy, low self-esteem, denial, anger and unforgiveness can become deadly and debilitating. They not only impair us mentally, but physically and emotionally as well. Over the next chapters, we will explore these and other issues at length. Freedom from the pain and guilt associated with these emotions will usher in the breakthrough needed to soar in every area of our lives. This pivotal change will take faith so that we may lay aside the weight that so easily overcomes us.

"Therefore, since we are surrounded by such a great cloud of witnesses, let us throw off everything that hinders and the sin that so easily

entangles. And let us run with perseverance the race marked out for us,

fixing our eyes on Jesus, the

pioneer and perfecter of faith. ..." (Hebrews 12:1, 2, *NIV*)

God is prepared to walk with you through this process of renewal. Whether you have an inflated or deflated ego, He wants to take you further. In either instance, life's circumstances have contributed tainted information regarding your self-worth and that has consequently developed what I call a "bound ego." A bound ego presents itself as prideful or self-debasing. These feelings frame how we approach life and how we see ourselves. A bound ego can also easily grow into a victimized spirit where it appears everyone is either doing things to us or keeping us from those things that are rightfully ours. In both cases, you must seek and receive deliverance to walk in the freedom we inherited by becoming a

child of God. It is your birthright!

Like most royals, you didn't join in, you were born into the lineage of Jesus Christ. Your inheritance gives you the blood- bought right to receive the complete inheritance listed in His "Will and Testament" – the Bible. This powerful birthright has been waiting for you all along. It is time for you to claim

it!

Change is more than a desire; real change takes work and determination! You must be willing to fight the internal argument that constantly tries to stop you from moving forward. While your heart may be cheering you on, your mind may try to make you feel unworthy, unprepared, or unable to take the road less traveled. Change is gained in baby steps. It will help you gain momentum to overcome the daily struggle where your own inner voices echo issues from your past that may cause you to feel like a victim.

Real, lasting change, the spirit-building kind of change, only comes when the victim spirit is brought into subjection of the Holy Spirit. Some of us have been wrestling with these spirits for so long, we begin to think that it's us. To overcome, we must first acknowledge and then put a stop to the areas of our chosen retreat that push us toward the victim mentality. Then, and only then, will we be able to overcome the victim spirit.

The Victimized Spirit

"As it is written: "For your sake we face death all day long; we are considered as sheep to be slaughtered."

No, in all these things we are more than conquerors through him who loved us." (Romans 8: 36, 37, *NIV*   )

1. The Victim of Rejection and Violation: One out of every 6 American women has been the victim of an attempted (2.8%) or completed (14.8%) rape in her lifetime. In addition, 17.7 million American women have been victims of molestation or attempted rape. But this crime is not gender specific. Nearly 3% of American men (1 in 33) have also experienced an attempted or completed

rape in their lifetime.

These crimes have become an epidemic. Yet, there are far more victims who will never report their abuse. Sex-crime victims are more likely to suffer from depression, post-traumatic stress disorder (PTSD), substance abuse and suicidal ideation. Not surprising, victims are represented in every demographic, culture, ethnicity and most every family.

Crimes like these were also common during biblical times. They were probably more prevalent in those days because there were no laws or punishment to regulate such behavior. One such account can be found in Genesis Chapter 34 about a girl named Dinah, the daughter of Leah and Jacob. Leah was the victim of her husband's rejection. Jacob, because he did not love her. He loved her sister, Rachel.

It was Jacob's desire to marry Rachel. However, the girls' father, Laban, tricked Jacob into marrying Leah, who was not at all attractive. He told Jacob that if he worked for him seven years, he could have Rachel's hand in marriage. Jacob agreed, but after the time had passed, Laban went back on his word and gave him Leah to marry instead. Though he had no interest in Leah, he agreed to take her and work another seven years to marry the love of his life, Rachel. So, it was. Jacob was the husband to both sisters. Throughout their lifetime, dissension and competition was constant between the two women.

Leah seemed to be a very loving and submissive wife to Jacob and bore him many children, which was customary. Despite her effort, Leah never felt like she mattered to Jacob. Nothing she did seemed to be enough to gain his love. Jacob preferred Rachel. He tolerated Leah. It was completely normal for a man to have more than one wife in those days. But can you imagine what it must have been like to have the same husband as your sister? Leah did not feel she mattered, and it became her reality. Unfortunately, she passed a generational curse on to her daughter, Dinah. Since she was raised in the middle of all this, I would imagine that Dinah felt she didn't matter to her father any more than her mother did.

Dinah was beautiful, tall, and sinewy, yet graceful. At the age of 14, she was considered ready for marriage according to the village elders, yet she was very childlike as most teens are. She was free-spirited, headstrong, and independent. Dinah took great pleasure in tormenting her twelve older brothers by chasing the sheep and goats they tended. The playful type, Dinah especially loved to startle the goats which sent her brothers chasing after them. She also loved to eavesdrop on adult conversations, particularly Canaanite women who were married. Leah was a Hittite and had been advised to stay away from these women as they were considered "unclean." Yet, Dinah's curiosity pursued more. She loved to hear their juicy gossip.

Shechem, a handsome young man, and the son of the ruler, was out riding his horse one day, when he spotted Dinah. He was immediately drawn to her. Shechem was like a prince, the local celebrity, so Dinah felt honored when he came to talk to her. This young man was older than Dinah by at least ten to fifteen years, and he was very handsome. Dinah became a little nervous because men did not talk to young women for any length of time without first gaining their father's permission. During that time, girls were required to be accompanied by other women while talking to a man.

"When Shechem son of Hamor the Hivite...saw her, he took her [Dinah] and raped her." (Genesis 34:2, *NIV*) She felt a stabbing pain between her legs as Shechem pushed himself inside of her. Not only was this a violent situation, it was extremely painful because Dinah was a virgin. Like any woman who is the victim of this type of violation, I'm sure that this 14 year- old girl demanded him to stop! But Shechem continued until he was satisfied. Dinah's screams for help were unheard or perhaps ignored. After all, Shechem was powerful. Dinah was just a girl with no real importance; she didn't matter.

Shechem's uncontrollable desire for Dinah not only dishonored her, but her family as well. The Bible says that Shechem *loved* her (v. 3) and asked his father to secure her as his wife (v.4). However, if he had been an honorable man, he would have asked Dinah's father for her hand in marriage first. Instead he allowed himself to be used by the enemy. Dinah was physically, emotionally, and spiritually dead inside. Because of this terrible misfortune, the flower of her youth was destroyed and her destiny endangered. This type of violence carries with it, eternal consequence.

Dinah was tormented by nightmares. I'm sure hearing Canaanite women talk about their sexual exploits was no longer of interest. Dinah, once confident, likely experienced long-term depression. If she didn't feel she mattered before, she certainly didn't feel she mattered now. This devastating moment became the circle where she stood for a very, very long time.

But this wasn't the end of Dinah's story. The God of Israel heard her cry, saw her pain, and redeemed her honor. When Dinah's brothers heard what happened to their sister, *"...they were shocked and furious, because Shechem had done an outrageous thing..."* (v. 7). Shechem was willing to pay any price for Dinah to become his wife.

38

However, Dinah's brothers deceitfully negotiated a deal with Shechem and Hamor. Since they and *every* man in their tribe, were circumcised, they demanded that Shechem and all the men in his tribe become circumcised too. Every man was therefore circumcised. But while they were recovering, Dinah's brothers, Simeon, and Levi, killed every single man, took their wives and children, and confiscated all their possessions and wealth. In doing so, Dinah was vindicated, and her entire family and nation was blessed with generational wealth!

What a victory! Dinah became greater than her circumstance. God lifted her head from shame. Of all the daughters of Jacob, Dinah is the only one the Bible references by name. God turned her pain to promise. He fulfilled His Word and was with her even until the end. Our Heavenly Father orchestrated the rescue of this young girl even when it appeared, she did not matter. Is Dinah a victim? I don't think so. Dinah is a woman who mattered!

Through Dinah's story we learn that trusting God, even in trouble – when things are out of our control or when we are the victims of other people's decisions – the redemptive grace of God much more abounds. We may not have family members, friends or even our children to come to our rescue in a time of need, but Jesus is our intercessor. He goes to the Father on our behalf and He makes the same grace that was available to Dinah, available to each of us today.

2. The Victim of Hopelessness: Hannah was a beautiful young woman who married a prominent and eligible young man named Elkanah. He loved Hannah tenderly and she loved him with all her heart. Hannah was raised in an orthodox family and was taught to remain pure until marriage. She was obedient which made her parents happy. Her life was set; she married a rich, tall, dark, and handsome man. He was fine! Elkanah was desired by all the women and hated by all the men.

"Elk," as Hannah called him, had another wife, Penninah. It was customary of that time for a man to have as many wives as he could afford. A woman's value was determined by her ability to have children, especially male children. "Penny" was not particularly loved by Elk, but she was remarkably fertile and therefore of great value to him. Hannah had never given birth and was constantly reminded of this shortcoming because Penny constantly flaunted her sons and daughters. The Bible says, *"...the Lord had closed her womb."* (1 Samuel 1:6, *New King James Version*) Penny believed she should have been the most valued wife in the house, perhaps even the apple of Elk's eye.

Unfortunately, she was not: Hannah was.

Over time, Hannah became depressed because of Penny's insensitive cruelty.

Hannah stopped eating because the sorrow of her empty womb consumed her. Elk tried to reaffirm his love for her hoping it would take Hannah's mind off the fact that they had no children together, none of these things seemed to help

Hannah.

But Hannah had more on the inside than she realized; she would learn her way out was within! At the end of her rope, she was ready for change. Drastic circumstances required drastic action. In Hannah's spirit, she knew she had to come face to face with the only One who could turn her life around – God. She determined in her heart that no matter what it took, by faith, she was going to

move the hand of God.

The church she attended was subdued and quiet. Most of the communication with God was done by the priest and other everyone else remained relatively quiet. Realistically, Hannah just couldn't remain quiet any longer. As she approached the altar, it felt as if she was having an out-of-body experience. She no longer heard the prayers of the priest, Hannah had a singleness of heart and mind when she fell before the altar. In deep anguish and with hot tears rolling down her face, she stood up and began to pray. Though it was not audible, her lips were moving. The priest thought she was drunk. She reached out to the God of her fathers for a remedy that would ease her heartache and pain. She begged God to pull her out of the dungeon of despair which made her feel as though she didn't matter!

Was there no happiness for Hannah? Was there no child that would come from the womb of her body? She longed for life to kick inside of her. Wasn't it her time? She continued to speak and bombard Heaven even with the rebuke of the priest and others watching. *"And she made a vow saying, "Lord Almighty, if you will only look on your servant's misery and remember me, and not forget your servant but give her a son, then I will give him to the Lord for all the days of his life, and no razor will ever be used on his head."* (1 Samuel 1:11, *NIV*)

Thereafter, the priest spoke a blessing over her, *"...go in peace and may the God of Israel grant you what you have asked of him."* (v. 17) The Scripture goes on to say that Hannah ate a meal, her face changed, and she was no longer depressed. The Lord remembered Hannah. He spoke during a chaotic situation a word so full of promise that it ignited her womb, healed her pain, and propelled her toward destiny! Not only did Hannah give birth to Samuel, she gave birth to other children as well. The Word of God records that Samuel grew up in the presence of God and continued to grow in favor and in stature. Is Hannah a victim? I don't think so. Hannah is a woman who mattered!

There are many stressors that come into play when making life decisions. When we are faced with life decisions big or small most of us do our best to make the right choice. Yet there are times, despite our good intentions, we make poor choices. These choices are reflected in the people we hang around, the jobs we start or quit, how we spend money and even how we treat our bodies. Choices for most folks, regardless of their need, may be difficult in the best of situations because the greater the stress in deciding, the greater the setup for failure.

When the decision is going to bring us immediate gratification over our perceived need, we often choose poorly. Many people have such a high fear of failure that it negatively impacts their decision-making, often resulting in regret. Some scientific studies indicate that when we make decisions that we end up regretting, it influences our future brain activity.

Our brains don't forget the bad decision we have made. Instead our brains become hardwired with emotional memories of these experiences. This process shapes our future decisions.

Many studies have shown that the end of an experience, whether good or bad, has a greater influence on our future choices than the overall experience itself. It is human nature to choose immediate gratification, even when it equates to a poor choice. However, we have the power to make sound choices that change our direction and in the long run, our destiny.

God is not a respecter of persons; He will do the same thing for you and me that He did with Hannah. He turned her weeping into rejoicing. You may not be dealing with this issue, your issue could be related to your career, a broken relationship, or unforgiveness. The point is this: don't lose faith in God. Increase your faith as Hannah did, and watch Him show out on your behalf. He who promised is faithful!

3. The Victim of Poor Choices: There was a young woman who was raised in a pretty good family. She and her siblings were raised to have a strong sense of morals and values. When people spoke of this young woman, they labeled her based on her choice of profession, which was prostitute. Life has a way of presenting options that immediately gratify our needs and desires: whether that of our own or others.

This woman had a mystical look: a dark, olive complexion, long, black, wavy, hair and deep, coffee-brown eyes. The contrast of her hair and skin caused her eyes to sparkle and drew most men's attention. She was headstrong and usually made decisions without being influenced by others. Rahab was her name and it seemed to describe her destiny. The first part of her name "Ra" is the name of an Egyptian god. The second half, "hab" means *fierce*. Fierceness is the exact trait Rahab would later need to make a difficult choice that would change her destiny forever.

Rahab was an Amorite and her people served a pantheon (temple) of gods. Prostitution was encouraged in the temple of the god of fertility, and Rahab subscribed to the lifestyle of a harlot. Her home was on the outskirts of the city, so men could easily visit without being noticed. The house was far off the beaten path and was located near the wall that enclosed the city. Rahab had an outgoing personality and owned a reputable business of drying flax on her roof top. She dyed it various colors and sold her goods to local women for linen.

Because of Rahab's reputation as a prostitute, she likely believed it was all she would ever become. She gave herself to men who would never love her, nor regard her as someone who mattered. Therefore, in her mind there would be no knight in shining armor to save her from this life of despair and disappointment. Instead, after using her to gratify their needs, they left a few pieces of silver on the floor for her to collect as payment. Sure, she could have fine clothes, ride the best of chariots, and buy material things, but there was no lasting benefit to any of it. This non-gratifying lifestyle eventually left her lifeless because she participated in what should have been an "act of love" outside of marriage and therefore without receiving love in return.

Rahab, like many women today, hated her life and she hated herself for it. I'm sure she envisioned a better life, dreamed of someone better than a man who would take advantage of her, or some great opportunity that would grant her the power to change her life. How could she go on this way? She couldn't. God had a better plan of redemption. Out of nowhere and at the same time, out of everywhere, the God who stood above all the gods Rahab had served, made a move on her behalf and that of His people.

It was a typical night with familiar visitors who paid for her services. But something seemed different. It wasn't the wind. It wasn't the rising of the moon that shined so brightly. Rahab heard footsteps on her rooftop. When she peeked out her window, she saw two strangers. She could tell because they dressed and looked differently. She eventually learned they were spies sent by God to take her city.

Rahab beckoned them to come and hide in her home. The men complied. While they were there, Rahab told them all she heard about them leaving Egypt, the parting of the Red Sea and their conquests. The spy's shared the details of their exodus from Egypt and how their God parted the Red Sea allowing them to walk through on dry ground. Their eyewitness details gave Rahab Chills as they described how a group of people who had never been considered conquerors, overthrew the two kings, Sihon and Og. (Joshua 2:8-11)

Rahab was moved by all accounts. Here were two men, who were very different from all the other men who sought her company in the past. These men came seeking nothing but found protection when they needed it most. This became a turning point in Rahab's life. She recognized clearly that these men had a relationship with their God that she did not have with the gods she served. God Almighty had done miraculous things for them and she wanted to know the awesome God they served!

She also knew that sooner or later the king of Jericho would find out she was hiding spies. These were men of God on a mission, moving with passion to overthrow the enemies of their God. A God who skillfully set in motion the meeting of a harlot to complete His plan. God didn't wait for her to get herself together, or to become respectable. He had called her just as He has called you and I: while we were still sinners and doing our thang! God wants you to do something courageous, to walk into your predetermined destiny, just as Rahab did. She chose God!

Scripture says Rahab the harlot married Salmon, a prince of Judah and became a descendant of God's son, Jesus Christ. Rahab helped the spies to leave the city safely without being noticed and they promised her that when they returned with their army, she and her family would be saved from harm. They kept their word.

Although Rahab lived a life plagued with poor choices and labels, God intercepted her journey of destruction and turned it into a journey of destiny. She made a mark in life and in history that superseded her past. She mattered to God because she ushered in the Savior Who came to set us all free! You may be surprised to know that Jesus was a descendant of

Rahab. Is Rahab a victim? I don't think so. Rahab is a woman who mattered!

CHAPTER THREE

Victim? I Don't Think So!

"For the Spirit God gave us does not make us timid, but gives us power, love and self-discipline." (2 Timothy 1:7, *NIV*)

Most victims become intimidated with either actual or perceived problems. Some talk themselves into believing that they are okay, or that staying in a bad situation is best. There are those who spiritualize their circumstances by explaining that God wants them to suffer as Christ did. However, God has not given us a fearful spirit; He has given us a spirit that is powerful, loving and disciplined.

Although many people feel they have been victimized in some way, we cannot allow the victim mindset to become our home. Seeing ourselves as "less than" puts us in a position to allow people, situations, and circumstances to stagnate our power and growth. That is not in line with God's will for us.

As a minister, I counsel couples. Over the years, I have talked to battered spouses – men and women – who seem to easily justify that the physical and emotional abuse they have endured is alright. They try to convince me that the other person was just having a "bad day" or that they themselves were somehow at fault. In denial, or afraid of being honest, some adamantly proclaim the abuse has only happened once. Others have had the courage to admit being abused but have been deceived into believing that love will see them through. Although love can help, it is not enough to end the cycle of abuse. People need far more! Sometimes it takes years, or even decades to heal from the wounds of abuse. In abusive situations, it is not just the bruises or broken limbs that need healing, it is primarily the mind and spirit that need healing.

There are children who have fallen victim to a bullying sibling or schoolmate. Unfortunately, their parents were unaware, or failed to set the necessary boundaries to protect the child. In some cases, children are abused by parents who themselves were victims of abuse, and the cycle continues. There are also adults who become the victims of an overbearing or unjust boss simply because they need to pay their bills. Still others become the victims of church leaders who have convinced him or her that it is "biblical" to be submissive. While submission *is* a biblical principal, taking advantage of someone is not.

There are countless types of abuse and reasons behind it. Whenever we are deceived into cosigning or agreeing with untruths, we get out of alignment with God and in alignment with the enemy, who is the devil. He is the father of lies. If you are or have in the past been a victim of any type of abuse, you can

overcome the brokenness associated with this setback. In fact, if you are in an abusive situation right now, I encourage you to immediately seek help and protection.

Empowering Replacement Strategies

One way to begin the healing process is to denounce one lie at a time. We must replace hurt, hopelessness, defeat, and negative thinking – whether toward ourselves or others – with the power found in God's Word. Healing is not an easy fix and it doesn't happen overnight. It takes time and practice to exchange demeaning thoughts and dead-end attitudes for confident thoughts and positive attitudes. The outcome of relying on God and His Word is the blessing of power, love and a sound mind we receive

by including Him in the process.

To overcome the pain of being a victim, decide that you will invite God into the process. Pray, and seek Him with all your heart. These steps are necessary for long-term healing to begin: 1. Read the Word of God

2. Memorize the Word of God

3.Believe the Word of God

Make this process a habit. It is the secret to having a better life full of peace, healing, and progress. These three simple steps can help you get through any challenge you face or goal you set. The wealth of wisdom found in Scripture has the power to radically change your life!

Listed are three empowering keys that will help you overcome along with

Scriptures to help you start spending time with God daily. Begin your day

using the power of God's Word to breakdown the strongholds that have

tainted your spirit and delayed your destiny.

1.The Power of God's Word

God means what he says. What he says goes. His powerful Word is sharp

as a surgeon's scalpel, cutting through everything, whether doubt or defense, laying us open to listen and obey. Nothing and no one is

impervious to God's Word.

We can't get away from it, no matter what. (Hebrews 4:12,13,*MSG*)

Consequently, faith comes from hearing the message, and the message is

heard through the word about Christ. (Romans 10:17, *NIV*)

When your words came, I ate them −swallowed them whole. What a feast!

What delight I took in being yours, O God, God-of-the- Angel-Armies!

(Jeremiah 15:16, *MSG*)

For the flesh desires what is contrary to the Spirit, and the Spirit what is

contrary to the flesh. They are in conflict with each other, so that you are

not to do whatever you want. (Galatians 5:17, *NIV*)

Sanctify them by the truth; your word is truth. (John 17:17, *NIV*)

2. The Presence of the Fruit of the Spirit

The apostle, Paul, preached about the call of God to freedom. His message

is as relevant today as it was then. This is what he conveyed: *If we have*

accepted the freedom that only Christ provides, then we are done with the demands of this world! Now, we are free to live in the Spirit and to be truly right with God. When we are free, we rely on the Spirit to reveal to us the characteristics of Jesus. Like Him, we too, can freely love and experience joy and peace.

Through Christ we can display patience, kindness, and faithfulness. God expects us to reflect His goodness in the way we live, while at the same time being gentle and under control. The Fruit of the Spirit are *gifts*. As we grow in faith, we begin to better understand that we belong to God and possess His Spirit.

But the fruit of the Spirit is love, joy, peace, forbearance, kindness, goodness, faithfulness, gentleness, and self-control. Against such things there is no law. (Galatians 5:22, 23, NIV)

But the Advocate, the Holy Spirit, when the Father will send in my name, will teach you all things and will remind you of everything I have said to you. (John 14:26, NIV)

...for the fruit of the light consists in all goodness, righteousness, and truth. (Ephesians 5:9, NIV)

May the God of hope fill you with all joy and peace as you trust in him, so that you may overflow with hope by the power of the Holy Spirit. (Romans 15:13, NIV)

But you, man [woman] of God, flee from all this, and pursue righteousness, godliness, faith, love, endurance, and gentleness. (1 Timothy 6:11, NIV)

3. The Discipline of a Sound Mind

The end of all things is near. Therefore, be alert and of sober mind so that you may pray. forcefully. (1 Peter 4:7, NIV)

Deciding to strengthen certain areas of your life is a big step toward minimizing your struggles. You no longer have to be a victim of your circumstances. You are becoming all that God has prepared you to be, and you are victorious in Him!

The ability to live without limits is directly connected to how you think. If your thoughts are bankrupt, then the things you pursue in life will be empty and worthless. Our thoughts are a combination of learned skills and abilities; therefore, we can learn new skills. By changing how we think, we clear the way for more positive relationships and better decision-making. Through disciplined thoughts, we defeat the repetitive issues we deal with year in and year out. Attempting to lead our lives with a defeated and victimized mindset only causes problems, wastes time, and ultimately leads to frustration.

Every major life decision should be based upon the truths found in the Word of God. We make multiple decisions daily by withdrawing information we have placed in our minds. If the information we have received has been vile, self-defeating, or wrong, the choices we make will be faulty. When we use the ingested Word of God, it causes us to consider whether we are making decisions that are pleasing to God.

The Bible teaches us to guard our hearts. Why? Because out of it flow the issues of life. Issues are the things we concentrate on, think about often and at times, allow to consume us. Every action is preceded by thoughts. While we cannot control the things that pop up in our minds, we do have the power to prevent them from being our focus. God tells us that we must take every thought captive that opposes Him and His will. Don't allow random thoughts to cloud your mind, instead, reject them. In other words, if it's not right, get rid of it!

Your Mind and Life Reloaded

Do not conform to the pattern of this world but be transformed by the renewing of your mind. The you will be able to test and approve what God's will is—his good, pleasing, and perfect will. (Romans 12:2, NIV

Over the last few pages, you have begun the hard work of getting rid of old thoughts, stagnant beliefs, and fear. Now it is time to renew your soul. If you don't replace old habits and thoughts with something better, the old will soon return. This process begins with courage. Courage will help you overrule thoughts and actions that may cause you to slip into your old comfort zone.

Learning to love the way Christ loves us will require courage for sure. Love is the foundation by which we were created and therefore thrive. You can try living without love, but it is a very lonely place. You can even try to convince yourself that you will do just fine living without family and friends. But why would you deny yourself the joy that these relationships bring when God has so much more in store? (Yes, I know relationships can be trying and downright unbearable sometimes. However, you deserve the support and love of family, so take time to address the areas where healing is necessary so that you can enjoy your life with them.)

In some cases, it will mean forgiving people, both past and present, who have caused you harm. It is not the person, but the actions of the person that we struggle with most. The journey toward love begins with receiving the love the Creator has for you. In the Scriptures, He affectionately refers to His children as the apple of His eye and His beloved.

The truth is that our outward expressions reflect how we feel inwardly. Scripture teaches us that what we do and what we say mean absolutely nothing if the inward quality of love is void. By beginning to reload your mind and heart with what God says about you, the depth of His love will be revealed in greater magnitude than you ever thought possible.

In 1 Corinthians Chapter 13:4-8 (NIV), God defines love: Love is patient, love is kind. It does not envy, it does not boast, it is not proud. It does not dishonor others, it is not self-seeking, it is not easily angered, it keeps no record of wrongs. Love does not delight in evil but rejoices with the truth. It always protects, always trusts, always hopes, always perseveres. Love never fails....

Learning to love and accept yourself is perhaps the hardest change you will ever encounter, especially if you have never learned your value in God's masterful plan. Self-love adds balance. It produces self-healing and provides relational strength. Celebrate your victories and don't forget them. They will encourage you to keep going. Be thankful for how far you've come.

Live in Destiny Now

As you continue to renew your mind with God's Word, you will begin to see life through new lenses. The possibilities of what your life can be are endless! Think about that for a moment. By changing the way, you think and letting go of past hurt, disappointment and unforgiveness, you open the door to greater possibilities.

Here is a concept for your consideration. It is called "destiny living." Destiny living is "possibility living." If you have taken in everything offered from the previous chapters, you are beginning to realize how much you really matter. Day by day, you are moving toward what may have seemed before like a great impossibility. When you look in the mirror, begin saying, "I am more than a conqueror, and I am walking into my destiny!"

Let's look at two principles that will help you move further along this path of destiny. These principles are called "Destiny Knowledge (DK)." Destiny living supports your understanding by helping you to realize that the way you live is based on choice. It is not based on how others live, or how they think you should live.

DK Principle One: You Determine Your Attitude.

There will always be hardships to overcome, but how you face them is up to you. Decide that you will no longer give people or circumstances power over your life. Although you cannot control everything that happens, you can choose how you will respond. Your attitude frames how you think about things that happen to you. Remember, you are a victor not a victim. You have been given the power of the Holy Spirit and the gift of self-control. It is one thing to know that you have these options, but it is another to choose them when you are facing a challenge.

Here is an example: There were two men confined to a hospital room. One often complained about the white wall by his bed. He wanted a window like his roommate. Every day, the man whose bed faced the window took time to describe all the beautiful things that were happening outside his window. He described the radiant sunlight, the falling rain and the rainbow of flowers that grew as a result. The man described children rolling in rich green grass, butterflies dancing above the flowers and the majestic sound of hummingbirds and sparrows singing almost daily. The joy of seeing families laugh together and lovers holding hands made his heart leap. Hearing his roommate share such beautiful descriptions of the view, gave the man with no window sheer joy and calm. So much so, he would fall asleep as he imagined it all.

One day, the man with the window-view passed away. His roommate asked the nurse if he could have the bed by the window. She agreed and proceeded to make the change. Excited to see the view outside firsthand, he threw open the curtains only to find an old, disfigured wall. Dismayed, he wondered why his roommate had chosen to make up such stories rather than complaining about the ugly wall. He concluded that his roommate had intentionally chosen to imagine all that he wished he had rather than complaining about what he didn't have.

DK Principle Two: Replace Negativity with Positivity

Having a positive and hopeful attitude changes our outlook on life and its circumstances. Complaining weakens while hope encourages. ₁ The apostle Paul

suffered mistreatment and spent

1 DK Principle Two: Replace Negativity with Positivity

years behind bars. Despite it all, he made the choice to think positively rather than complain about his situation. He could have easily griped about everything that went wrong in his life and he would have been justified on some accounts.

Instead, Paul took the high road. He wrote many chapters of the Bible while incarcerated and continued to encourage himself by drawing closer in his relationship with God.

In Philippians 4:8, Paul gives us this practical advice: "Finally, brothers and sisters, whatever is true whatever is noble, whatever is right, whatever is pure, whatever is lovely, whatever is admirable – think about such things." (NIV) Likewise, I encourage you to follow Paul's example of demonstrating a positive attitude. Think the best about everything and everyone. Instead of focusing on your shortcomings or what you are lacking, give God praise for any and everything you can think of. Praise pushes you forward; negativity pulls you backward. I realize that embracing the destiny mindset is not easy. However, I know firsthand that it can be done.

The art of replacement (replacing old thoughts and attitudes with new, productive thoughts and attitudes) is a great way to overcome those moments when you are paralyzed by life's challenges. It is at those times that you can fill the spaces in your heart and mind with things that are true and lovely. It will usher you into a higher level of living. DK Principle Three: Discover Your

Purpose

"Each of you should use whatever gif you have received to serve others...." (1

Peter 4:10, NIV)

Knowing why God created you should be your greatest pursuit. You are not an accident. It was God's intention for you to be here at this time, in this place and for a predetermined purpose. Your personality, looks and talents are uniquely yours. No one else is an identical match. Every child of God has at least one gift and your responsibility is to find out what your gifts are and how God wants to use them for His glory.

Our Heavenly Father runs a successful business. His product is His people. Every child born into this family has a role in the business. God has given you specific gifts so that you may help others. At the root, love is the intention. When you operate from this prospective, He will prosper you to do more! There are some things that you just do naturally that others around you find difficult. These are gifts. If there is a burning desire in your heart to do something, whether it is small or so big that you can't imagine doing it, it is probably connected to your purpose. Consult God about next steps and decide that you

will keep going forward no matter what!

It is so important to use your gifts to bring glory and honor to our Heavenly Father. Misuse of your gifts is not only dangerous for others, but it can also be detrimental to you. When used wrongly or for personal gain, the same gift that provides comfort and assistance to many can become explosively destructive!

Your gifts are for the greater good of people and the greater glory of God. Knowing your gift gives your life purpose and direction.

Our ability to flow in the gifts God has granted is entirely up to us. Jesus and the early disciples freely used their gifts and like a magnet, people drew near to hear the Good News. When we feel the love of God flowing through us toward others, we are flowing in His overshadowing love for mankind. Pay attention to

God's still, small voice. He wants to lead you to your destiny. You matter to God and you are etched in His masterful plan. Embrace it!

CHAPTER FOUR

My Spirit Set Free

"So, if the Son sets you free, you are truly free."

(John 8:36, New Living Translation)

The previous chapters have uncovered ways that we can begin to take the chains (depression, unforgiveness, low self-esteem, the victim mentality, etc.) off our minds so that we can embrace the truth that we really do matter to God. To experience freedom in full; however, we must also allow the Spirit within us to be free. To embrace this realization, we must take the necessary steps to bring our mind into agreement with our spirit. This happens by hearing the Word of God continuously. We all have an intellectual understanding of what it means to be free, but until we know it in our spirit we will be bound.

So, how does the mind come into agreement with the spirit? It happens when we get to know God in an intimate way by spending time worshiping Him and seeking His face. God desires an intimate relationship with us. This has always been His plan since the creation of Adam and Eve. The Bible tells us that God walked through the garden and communed with them. As you increase your love for Him, His love will overtake you!

Building Your Relationship with God

Intimacy is established through prayer, worship and time spent in God's presence, but it involves more than you talking to Him. Prayer is an exchange between the two: you and God. The eye opener here is that God speaks, too. Practice sitting quietly and allowing the Heavenly Father to talk to you. Let Him pour His love on you. It is His love that will fill that longing in your heart to be loved and healed.

In the heart and spirit of every human being, there is a longing to be loved, healed, whole and free. God's love is the answer to everything you have been seeking to feel significant. Think about Who God is; He is the Creator of the universe! Look around you and you will see His magnificent craftsmanship. The very same God wants you to know Him intimately. He wants to spend quality time with you, and He has been with you in every situation from the very beginning.

Imagine being wrapped in the arms of God so tightly that you can hear His heartbeat. See that image in your mind and realize that type of closeness is possible with the Father, but you must actively work toward it. The more you spend time with Him, the closer to Him you will become. The less time you spend with Him, the further from Him you will become. He wants to reveal Himself to you in ways you can't imagine. If the God of the Universe desires intimacy with you, how could you possibly believe that you do not matter?

The Word says that God knew you before He formed you in your mother's womb! Even then, He had a plan for your life that would bring Him glory. If you are not doing so already, make up your mind to spend time with God daily.

I can promise you that anytime spent with Him will never be a waste of time. The mere fact that you are reading this book is a demonstration of God's love for you, because this message is intended to aid you as you make the next steps

in life.

A True Story on Forgiveness

I once met a woman who suffered with low self-esteem because of all the rejection she experienced. For the sake of this published work, we will refer to her as "Suzanne." As a young girl, she went to live with her aunt and uncle (also her godparents) who provided the stability her parents could not provide at the time. Suzanne would soon learn that her uncle was an alcoholic and her aunt was an enabler.

Suzanne's uncle converted the garage of their home into a sort of lounge. It was a comfortable room complete with a television and a full bar, and there was pornography paraphernalia everywhere! There were pornographic pictures hanging on the wall and magazines on the tables. This lounge was not only for her uncle's use, but it was also the place where Suzanne played with friends. Sadly, it was also the place where she was molested as a young girl by a friend of the family. She never told her aunt what happened because she was afraid, she would get in trouble. So, she held on to that secret.

This young girl held several secrets. For years, Suzanne had witnessed her father beat her mother without ever saying a word to anyone. She also held the secret that she had been molested several times. What it must have been like for a child to hold all those secrets. I can only imagine. She was so afraid, and yet she had no one to turn to. Suzanne's spirit was far from free because it was holding on to ultimate betrayals.

In time, Suzanne learned the importance of forgiveness and took the necessary steps to heal. She allowed God into the very places of her heart where mending was needed. She began to realize that God had been there when those terrible things happened, and He had been the One Who had wiped away the tears all those sleepless nights. By committing her life to

Christ and spending time with God often, she was eventually able to help others in need of emotional healing. Through prayer and worship, Suzanne was able to touch the heart of God and in turn, He touched and healed her brokenness.

Take Your Stand

God wants to set your Spirit free, too. The process begins when you make the decision to forgive yourself and others. I'm not sure what you've gone through in the past or what you may be going through now, but I encourage you to allow God's love to heal the areas that hurt. Set aside time with God each day. Turn off the television, put aside work and infiltrate the environment by listening to worship music. Ignite the atmosphere with words of gratefulness and speak transparently with God as you would a friend.

Each moment you spend in God's presence will propel you to a new level of freedom in your spirit! Before you know it, you will begin looking forward to getting away from the hustle and bustle of life to be alone with Him. No longer will you feel the need to seek people and things to fulfill you. There will come a day when you will be completely in love with God. He has chosen you to be used for His glory.

God values exactly who you are, and He accepts you and everything about you – even your mistakes and insecurities. He has been with you through every trial all the time knowing that you would come to the point of realizing how much you need Him. Make no mistake about it, you are important to God!

Whatever setbacks and disappointments you have experienced, please know that you are not alone. The enemy often tries to convince us that our situation is worse than everyone else's or that God has more important things to do than deal with our small problems. He is a liar! There are people who have gone through far worse things than you have and never lived to tell about it. You survived, and you have earned the privilege of having a great testimony. God protected you through the storms of life. You are in your right mind, and you are valued!

If you need one more reassurance that God finds you valuable, here it is: He died to save YOUR life! If you had been the only person on the planet, He still would have chosen to die for you.

Through the death of His Son, the Lord declared freedom over your life! Accepting it is your choice. God is never forceful; He won't force freedom on you. The Bible says, "Christ has set us free to live a free life. So take your stand! Never again let anyone put a harness of slavery on you." (Galatians 5:1, MSG) Likewise, I encourage you to take your stand for freedom! Say it, believe it, portray it ... you are free through Christ Jesus!

Break the Chains That Bind You

In our day and age, the thought of slavery is like watching an old movie. It just doesn't seem real that anyone would be enslaved today. But there is a type of slavery that exists beyond the physical chains of bondage. I am suggesting the type of slavery where people exercise control over another. Sometimes we are slaves to other people without even knowing it.

Meet "LaShawn," a beautiful young woman and her husband, "Steve." They have two children. The family joined a local church one summer, Sunday *morning. Pastor "Smith" had delivered an excellent message, with his usual rhythmic cadence accompanied by the soulful singing of the church choir.*

It wasn't long after that LaShawn began getting involved in the women's ministry, working alongside one of the founding mothers of the church, "Katherine Jones." Stout, matronly and over-nurturing, Mother Jones subtly began manipulating LaShawn under the pretense of "love." Mother Jones advised LaShawn how to pray, dress and listen to a particular type of music.

LaShawn considered their relationship special and she really wanted to please Mother Jones.

It didn't take long before LaShawn was totally overtaken by this woman's spirit of control. LaShawn couldn't do anything without Mother Jones' approval. When LaShawn was younger, she felt the call on her life to become a missionary and to minister to other women. When she shared her dream with Mother Jones, she disapproved. She had a different plan for LaShawn's life and Mother Jones fully intended to hold her to it, regardless of her dream.

When people call you to a position, you are bound by their call, but when God calls you there is freedom to pursue it! For a time, LaShawn submitted to Mother Jones' plan for her life. Mother Jones plan involved

LaShawn being her personal assistant by carrying her books, getting her water and responding to her demands. LaShawn's gift and vision were being held hostage by Mother Jones.

But God was faithful to LaShawn. He spoke to her heart and provided a friend to encourage her to break the stronghold she had endured at the hands of Mother Jones. Despite this hurtful experience in her past, LaShawn is becoming all that God called her to be. She accepted the freedom only God can provide. Today, she is fulfilling the will of God through missions and by empowering women.

How about you? Is there someone controlling your life? Your will? Your destiny? If so, take back the reigns over your life! No one deserves to be controlled by another. Even God gives us the freedom to choose the path we will take in life.

The apostle John teaches that there is no fear in love. Love has the power to drive away every fear that we will ever encounter (1 John 4:18a). God's love for us is not based on who we are, rather it is based on Who He is. His love is, therefore, perfect! Nothing can separate us from the love He has toward us. God doesn't turn away from us because of our weaknesses, dysfunction, or decisions.

I like to think of God as the Great Exchange Artist. By that I mean, He exchanges everything we have working against us for the things we need so that He may work through us: For weakness, He provides strength. For shame, He provides acceptance. For sickness, He provides healing. For pain, He provides joy everlasting! And the list goes on. When you receive this truth in your spirit, you will no longer fear acceptance or worry about whether you qualify. You are both accepted and pre-qualified by the Creator!

The perfection of God's love for you has the capacity to fill every empty space, elevate every low feeling, and fill your love tank to overflowing! God's love causes you to walk in victory for through every battle that life throws at you. This is the abundant life where nothing is impossible to those who believe.

Freedom is more than just a word or feeling. It is a journey in your mind and spirit to imagine the unimaginable. It is coloring outside the lines if you will. You see, God has more in store for you than what you have been working toward. Remember, His thoughts are higher than our thoughts. He wants to do exceedingly more!

Answering the Call

No matter what God has called you to do, it will always seem too big to accomplish. So, if you're thinking about what God has spoken to you and it seems too big, join the club. Look at it this way. The job God has called you to isn't impossible to achieve, however, the only way to accomplish it is through His intervention. That means God must lead the way. His plan is more than you can think or imagine and will cost more than you can ever pay. I know you're thinking right now, "This elephant is huge!" Trust me, I understand. Just take one bite at a time. One letter...one call...one decision. It just takes one step of faith to get God involved. This is His plan, just say "yes" to His will and begin.

It is God Who orders your steps, not your stride! That's why some folks are further along than others. They took the freedom call of God and hit the ground running to follow His lead. Listen intently to His still, small voice so that He may direct your next step. God has your entire life mapped out. But to get to the place He has prepared, you must trust Him with your all! David provided a great response to God's call in Psalm 34:1-8 (MSG):

I bless God every chance I

get; my lungs expand with

his praise. I live and

breathe God ; if things

aren't going well, hear

this and be happy:

2   *Join me in spreading the news; together let's get the word out.*

3   *God met me more than halfway, he freed me from my anxious*
    fears.

4   *Look at him; give him your warmest smile. Never hide your*
    feelings from him.

5   *When I was desperate, I called out,*

and God got me out of a tight spot.

6   *God 's angel sets up a circle   of protection around us while*

we pray.

7   *Open your mouth and taste, open your eyes and see— how good*
    God is.

Blessed are you who run to him....

There is such power in your "yes" to God. Even when you are not sure about what to do next, just say "yes." By answering this way, you are declaring that you agree with God. It has been my experience that God rarely reveals where He is ultimately taking us. Yet, run to Him! He will empower you to do the seemingly impossible. It all lands on trust. Trusting God keeps you buoyant in the ocean of life. Before you leap, you must trust you will rise. The ability to rise is not based on your leap; but on your trust in the One Who keeps you from

falling.

Fundamental Fact of Faith

The single act of entrusting God to lead you to success, is a huge factor in turning your life around. It can be the beginning of turning a hopeless situation or relationship around if you will allow it. The Bible says, "The fundamental fact of existence is that this trust in God, this faith, is the firm foundation under everything that makes life worth living. It's our handle on what we can't see.

The act of faith is what distinguished our ancestors, set them above the crowd." (Hebrews 11:1, 2, MSG)

The fundamental fact of faith changes everything! The act of faith causes us to trust even when there is no evidence that we should. Our eyesight helps us by clearly bringing into focus things around us. The same is true with faith as it relates to the unseen aspects of the spiritual world. Faith brings into focus the reality of what is unseen.

Faith is understood through the Spirit alone. It is more than what you sense or feel. It cannot be measured or determined by some external test. Faith has its roots in trust, and trust gains its growth in faith. So then, trust allows us to believe that which is not readily seen. Trust may conflict with our natural tendency toward reasoning, and it will certainly leave logic questioning. Therefore, it must be practiced often.

Value, Worth, and Cost

The Oxford Dictionary defines value as "the importance, worth, or usefulness of something or to consider (someone or *something) to be important or beneficial.*" However, our value is not based on this worldly perspective. It is based on this selfless act of God: *"For God so loved the world, that he gave his only begotten Son, that whosoever believeth in him (Jesus)should not perish but have everlasting life. "*(John 3:16, *KJV*)

Value then equals worth. Worth drives cost. When you begin your quest toward discovering self-worth, you must consider the perspective you have of yourself. You can choose to be your own best friend or your worst enemy. It really doesn't matter as much what others feel about you, because you are always the number one guest on your list. When no one else is around, there you are. For this reason, you should aim to establish a healthy perspective.

Self-value is not the same as self-esteem, although people use them interchangeably. Self-esteem is rooted in confidence, well- being and admiration. It is developed by caring for your physical appearance as well as your mental and emotional health. When we lack self-esteem, we initiate self-suffering. On the other hand, self- value is established from the inside out. Most of us tend to place more care in how we appear outwardly – clothing, accessories, hair, nails, etc.

What use is it to appear beautiful on the outside, while our emotional and mental health is failing inwardly? Eventually the internal catches up with the external. We can see evidence through the outward signs of premature aging, weight gain, weight loss, skin irritation, brittle hair and the list continues. Since self-value grows from within, it is the part that we alone can control. That means that we can determine who deposits or withdraws from our sense of worth. This includes our loved ones and employers. We must give each the permission to enter our emotional bank.

Some folks are extremely open to external voices. They allow others to set standards, rules and boundaries for them. When we allow our lives to be run by external sources, we are basing our self-worth and ultimately our future on a slippery slope. Outside sources are not reliable. They are unpredictable and can change at will. Many times, the people who we allow to dictate our direction suffer from low self-worth themselves. Be sure your hope is built on Jesus Christ. In doing so, you will establish a strong foundation that can weather life's storms.

You are one-of-a-kind! Don't fall into the trap of comparing yourself to others. Using someone else's standards to live by is a sure way to overlook your personal worth and miss out on God's amazing plan for your life. Build your own standards to live by. Learn the art of failing forward by embracing mistakes and learning from them. Don't allow mistakes to lead to long-term anxiety or depression. Be frustrated! Be disappointed! Be angry if you chose, but don't stay there and wither! The more we learn from our missteps, the further ahead we get. There is no way to go back and recover one day we have lost! Hindsight is always the best! Although we cannot change our mistakes, we can change how we view them. Try seeing failure as a learning experience. Develop self-directed questions to discover what caused the mistake. This will empower you to make necessary changes so that you don't repeat the same outcome repeatedly.

Embrace the idea of being an ever learner. Consistently seek opportunities to improve who you are and elevate your possibilities. Engage in groups with like-minded people, attend conferences or find a new hobby. Meditate, read, and pray. Trying just one of these things will increase your self-esteem and improve your self-worth.

You may also want to consider finding a mentor, someone who can help you establish goals to move forward. A mentor can also serve as an accountability partner by helping you to frame your thoughts so that you can stay connected to your faith. Or use your experiences to impart wisdom into someone else's life. This simple act offers great rewards for you and for the other person. It also helps you take your focus off the negative things that have happened in your life.

No matter where you are in your journey, embrace the quest for self-worth. You can do this by keeping your emotional, mental, and spiritual closet clean of clutter. It is impossible to lift others if we have not taken the time to lift ourselves. You can only encourage them to a point. But when you teach them to invest in themselves, by being transparent about the steps you also take to maintain a high sense of worth, you empower them to grow through life's twists and turns.

Developing and honoring your personal value is the catalyst for your success! The ability to embrace who you are stretches your potential to become all that you believe. It also enables others to acknowledge your value. This remarkable exchange between yourself and others is the groundwork for exceptional growth, potential wealth, and believability. This is the measure of who you are and who you shall become.

There is a certain cost that accompanies growth and well- being. It is an investment in not only who you are today, but who you will become tomorrow. The investment will cost you your time, talent, and great effort. Surrender your all to God and place yourself on the altar of self-growth so that you can become all that God has created you to be. The cost of building self-value is available to everyone, but only those who strive for better reap the benefit of their investment.

CHAPTER FIVE

Work on the Inside Strengthens the Outside

In the previous chapter, I covered personal value and worth. Now, I want to spend some time focusing on what you believe inwardly and what you demonstrate outwardly. It is important that we always have a solid belief system. When we fail to establish and live by a certain belief system, we encounter consequences that cause us to circle around the same old issues again and again. The outcome is that our path toward destiny and fulfillment with be altered, denied, or delayed. The Bible teaches that we should let the mind of Christ live inside of us. To that end, we must bring every thought and idea into alignment with Christ's example.

Most folk ignore or take their belief systems for granted. They sail through life hoping to navigate the ocean to make it to the proverbial shore. While that approach might work for a while, they ultimately discover that their lives are empty, and their plans are off track. A healthy belief system gives us a foundation for true self-value and self-worth.

We can classify our value or worth as a set of rules or boundaries that define how we process and store information. This set of rules also establishes how we behave and our expectations of others. Without a solid belief system, particularly one founded on godly principles, our esteem is threatened, and our thoughts are unstable. The conscious mind devises a set of questions that guide our decision making about everything! As these questions develop, it is our belief system that dictates whether we will enjoy the blessings of a balanced, focused life or a frustrated, fearful, and misguided life.

Emotions and Beliefs

In 2015, Pixar created the animated movie, *Inside Out*. It dealt with the conflicting emotions of a young girl named Riley. Like all of us, she was guided by her emotions. In the movie, the character's emotions lived in what was known as "Headquarters," which was really her mind. Guided by emotions, Riley struggled to adjust to a new life in San Francisco. The idea of relocating to a new house, new school and new friends made life tough for Riley at the time. Although joy, Riley's primary emotion, attempted to redirect negative thoughts to positive, the other emotions created conflict that made the adjustment difficult. Over time, joy overruled the other emotions, but Riley had to work hard to adapt and return to her naturally positive mindset.

Get Your Emotions in Check

Like Riley, we too have primary emotions that advise us throughout the day. Whether it is a positive or negative emotion, it controls the way we think, act and respond. However, we have the final say-so on which emotion we allow to dominate. Think for a moment: which emotion is controlling your life right now? If it is a negative emotion, such as fear, distrust, or regret, decide that you will exchange it for a positive emotion that can move you closer to success.

Growth Strengthens Belief

When you were born, you established boundaries with your parent's help and the use of your senses. You learned basics like hot and cold, soft and hard, bright and dark. As you grew, you expanded those rules to include nice and funny, sad, and mad. This set of values worked for you then, but eventually you learned that you needed to establish rules concerning your interactions with people, circumstances, and other aspects of life.

What I am asking you now is to evaluate your emotions and belief system, then fine-tune areas where change is needed. Grab your journal or paper and pen. Determine what you value, not what you like or choose. Think about the emotions that drive you to act or think a certain way. What value system or emotions do you use when making decisions during difficult times and good times? What about your career? What thought processes guide you in furthering your career or pursuing your dreams? How much of a role do you give your family and friends in helping you navigate life? These are just a few questions to help you get started. Categorize different areas of your life and write the emotions or beliefs that guide you.

The emotions and beliefs you listed play a tremendous role in establishing your core. The foundation of everything you think is based on this core. Going through this process will help you clarify what is important and what refinement you will need to redirect your life from this day forward.

Sometimes we create a faulty set of rules that develop through our experiences. Honestly, when we evaluate ourselves, we sometimes find that what we once believed, is no longer the way we believe now. This could be the result of growth or regression. Some of our thoughts, though not intentional, are based on lies, deception and manipulation. They cause us to believe we have no value, can never be loved or that we will always be alone. You may be hearing negative self-talk as well. These negative and self- destructive set of rules must be redefined.

Unaware, we sometimes fail to adjust our belief system as we grow. For instance, if a person grew up in lack, everything they do now is most likely based on survival. Thoughts such as these prevail: *Will I have enough? I can't afford this or that? I will never have enough.* Some actions associated with this mindset include hoarding, being self-centered or always feeling someone is trying to take advantage. Every year we should assess and readjust our mindset, especially if our thoughts are defeating our progress. Continuing to live with a negative set of rules and antiquated ideas will not sustain us as we reach for the next level. We must boldly push them out and exchange them for new rules that
align with where we are currently headed in life.

This process can be difficult if you fear change. If that is the case, take control over your emotions! Initiate positive self-talk. Remember that when setting your new belief system, you must be rational, not emotional.

Begin with what you believe about God and your relationship with Him. It is on this sure foundation that we live, move and have our being. If you are unsure, you will not be able to move forward until you establish a basis for the most important relationship in your life. By working through this area, you will be better able to handle future experiences that may attempt to hinder you. Problems lose their potency when they come in contact with the shadow of the Almighty!

The Believability Factor

Belief and faith run hand in hand. They are two sides of the same coin, and creators of the intersection between growth and answered prayers. The Bible declares that without faith (a belief system based on God's Word) it is impossible to please God. Growing in faith does not have to be a struggle. Receive it as a gift that comes from God through grace. God gives grace freely when we meet His conditions. *What are the conditions?* Glad you asked! Ephesians 2:8-9 says it this way, "For it is by grace you have been saved, through faith − and this is not from yourselves, it is the gift of God − not by works, so that no one can boast." (*NIV*)

Faith or belief is not something we can think into existence outside the grace of God. That type of belief is weak and will only last for a short period. If your belief is purely based on emotion and logic, then faith becomes something self-generated based on your own thoughts rather than God's will. When you concoct your own belief system outside of the will of God, it may be believable to you, but it lacks the power and authority that comes only from God.

Concocted faith is all in your mind and is not supported by God at all. The faith God gives is supernatural and establishes a strong cornerstone of belief. Because it is from God, this faith is alive and active in your day-to-day life. It infiltrates your mind and spirit. It is foundational and comes by hearing and receiving God's Word in your heart. Faith is the commerce of God. With faith comes the promises of God. With faith comes guidance, stability, trust, and believability.

Discipline: A Necessary Component

The next step in redefining your belief system is to apply discipline. This step will help you gain control, trust your decisions, and clarify the direction for your life. It is time to establish relationships based on trust and believability. Once your belief system is established and rooted in godly principles, your relationships will grow. People will see you as credible. When you align your faith with God's Word, you project a certain level of personal strength that others can believe in. Your self-confidence and self-worth increase exponentially!

"Self-trust is the first secret of success...the essence of heroism." ~ Ralph Waldo Emerson

Building trust or believability is easier said than done. Do you find it strange that you can often trust other people more than you trust yourself? All other people have to do is look official, wear a white jacket and we'll allow them to check places we won't allow our closest loved ones to venture. People can make a video, post it on social media and claim to have the latest and greatest diet solution and we will purchase their "bubble gum diet!" It is amazing how trusting we can be.

Let's take a closer look. Ask yourself: *Do I usually seek the opinions of others first before I make a move?* If you are like most folks, you fluctuate between trusting your thoughts and waiting for someone else to qualify your direction. A speaker posed a question to a group of renowned leaders in business, finance, government and education. She asked, *"If you had to make an important decision and the information told you one thing, but your intuition and gut strongly told you another. What would you do?"* Most leaders stated they would gather more data and likely follow their gut! In essence, they had a deep trust for their own decision-making.

How is this type of trust developed? Psychologist Carl Rogers developed an approach called the *Humanistic Approach*. His premise was that a person must develop a positive self-regard to improve their instincts and judgment. When this occurs, there is no great need to rely on the opinions of others in decision-making. To increase one's ability in this way, a person must carefully choose the words he or she thinks and says about self. Positive, honest communication is the key.

As you gain momentum toward more solid decision-making, re-evaluate your goals or set new ones. Most of us like to set high, lofty goals that can at times be unrealistic. We take a few steps, then we fall off the wagon because things aren't happening fast enough. Don't get me wrong. I'm not saying that we should minimize our goals, I'm just saying that our goals are more likely to be realized when we marginalize the larger goal by breaking it into bite-sized pieces. It's like making a New Year's resolution to lose fifty pounds. If you lose five pounds the first month, keep going and celebrate every five. Before you know it, those fifty pounds will be gone! The same is true in all forms of goal setting. With each conquest, you move one step closer to the larger goal.

To Thine Own Self Be True

Be true to yourself. Don't be afraid for people to see the real, authentic you. It takes real strength to be vulnerable; it is not a weakness. Step out with faith and confidence. Don't be overly concerned with what people think of you or the goals you have set for your life. You will fall occasionally, and it's okay to admit, "Hey, I missed it that time." Just be sure to get back up again.

"Vulnerability sounds like truth and feels like courage. Truth and courage aren't always comfortable, but they're never weakness."

~ Brene Brown

Being vulnerable was once very difficult for me. Early in my childhood, I lived in a very poor neighborhood. Our economic status was considered by some, vulnerable or weak. As children, we had to put on a false face and pretend so that no one would take advantage of us. When my family moved to a better area, I realized that some of the traits of survival that I had previously used to protect myself had closed me off to important relationships. By that I mean, instead of being open and friendly to the new people I met, I was guarded and suspicious. In certain situations, I would act like I had it all together, when in reality, I needed help from others around me. I thought that if they knew I needed them, they would mistreat me or take advantage of me.

The very concepts that I am sharing with you in this book are the steps I took to create a positive perspective on life. I became okay with accepting help when I needed it, without thinking less of myself or worrying that others would think less of me. I understand that I cannot be vulnerable with everyone, but the level of freedom I have gained by taking the pressures off, has given me an entirely new reality and with it, great peace.

We open ourselves to explore new things and develop new skills when we come to grips with the truth about vulnerability. That is what happened to me. Initially, I thought to be vulnerable meant I had to be submissive or weak, but that's not what it meant at all. The courage to be our authentic selves is developed through this type of vulnerability. Yes, there is a level of uncertainty, risk and emotional exposure involved. It is only natural for us to guard our deepest desires and avoid being trampled upon or rejected. Please don't think I am saying this is an easy process. It is not. On the same token, neither am I suggesting that we can open ourselves to just anyone. As with all things, balance and discretion must be exercised.

It is through difficult experiences that every encounter in our lives are framed. Painful experiences become the measuring rod we use to determine whether our shield of rejection remains on high alert or not! If people get too close or are too loving, our subconscious alarm sends a warning signal to our mind flashing memories of past hurt. Fear then hinders us from fully enjoying the incredible benefits of a new friendship or romantic relationship.

Often past hurt keeps us from being open. After all, it may have been our vulnerability that led someone to mistreat or betray us. I get that. We've all been hurt. Some people have a laundry list of reasons that prevent them from being open and honest with others. But to reap the benefits of lifelong, meaningful relationships, some level of vulnerability is required. Therefore, carefully consider when and with whom you can be vulnerable. Remember, the journey to change always begins on the inside before it is evident on the outside.

"Give me understanding so that I may keep your law and obey it with all my heart."

(Psalm 119:34, *NIV*)

Embrace the Authentic

It doesn't matter how sound your mind may be the beliefs you hold from past experiences form your present reality. These beliefs tend to cloud our perception. Vulnerability is truly the key to lasting relationships. C.S. Lewis said it best, "To love at all is to be vulnerable." Steps toward vulnerability can be evident in your willingness to lower your guard by allowing people to see the real you. It means daring to show the authentic you! Yes, the you that you're not altogether happy with yet. The you that disagrees with your appearance − how tall or short you are, the color of your hair or skin, and all the other aspects you will eventually learn to embrace!

Being authentically you is an ever-evolving process. This is no overnight endeavor. It absolutely will take time and you will have to be intentional in putting the principles discussed in this chapter into practice. Take the time to evaluate your life, your relationships, and your aspirations. Make sure they are in line with God's will. You may find that a few changes are necessary. It is okay. Embrace this higher level of living by listening to your spirit, and by living with intention. In a world where everything and everyone is trying to make you conform, stand your ground!

You have been called to a life of authenticity. Learn to embrace who you are today while remaining open to who you are becoming with God's help. He is working through everything in your life: the good, bad, hurt and

disappointment. He can use everything you've experienced to bring you to your destiny. Everything He has created is beautiful. You are no exception. You are a Designer's original and you are good enough.

CHAPTER SIX

Acting Out Is Not an Act at All

"A person without self-control is like a city with broken-down walls."
(Proverbs 25:28, *NLT*   )

You can't talk yourself out of a problem you've behaved yourself into.

Stephen R. Covey

My parents were big on discipline. We learned early on to exercise self-control and to avoid impulsive reactions at all cost. My mother used to say, "If you can't control yourself, you can't control anything!" Having well-mannered children was her life goal. She was one of very few women who could bring all eight of her children to a meeting or church program and feel confident that we would be respectful, quiet and still. However, as I got older, I realized that many of my friends lacked this type of discipline. I had a friend in college named "Linda." At first glance, she seemed quiet and demure. One afternoon, we decided to go to the mall to shop. Linda drove. California has busy highways and that day was no different. The roads were congested, and drivers were jockeying in and

99

out of lanes trying to gain a better vantage point. Linda had to slam on her breaks a few times to avoid a potential accident. Before long, Linda was visibly irritated and to my surprise began yelling out a few choice words and giving them the finger. It was crazy!

When we finally arrived, she noticed how quiet I was and asked if I was okay. I told her that I was fine, but that I never expected her to lose it like that! Of course, she justified her actions, but my mother's old saying began to ring very clearly in my head. Linda had not exercised control and it could have cost us our lives.

Self-discipline is one of the most important tools for self- improvement, a catalyst for achieving personal success. By exercising discipline, we are better equipped to manage our emotions, overcome fear, depression and even addiction. It helps us to stay quiet when we are bursting inside with words we want to say.

Success becomes more attainable when we make the best choice despite the way we feel. The Scripture says, "Be careful what you say and protect your life. A careless talker destroys himself." (Proverbs 13:3, *Good News Translation*) People who have learned self-discipline, choose their words carefully because the power of life and death is in the words they speak.

Part of learning the skill of self-discipline is knowing our limits: understanding what we can and cannot take. When we are disciplined, people can't push our buttons and provoke us like they used to either. The Bible teaches, "If you are sensible, you will control your temper. When someone wrongs you, it is a great virtue to ignore it." (Proverbs 19:11, *GNT*)

Learning self-discipline has countless benefits. These are just a few:

It helps you to keep self-destructive behaviors in check.

It enables you to find balance in your life.

It eliminates feelings of helplessness or co-dependence on others. It helps you refrain from emotional responses.

It helps you to remove negativity and gain peace of mind.

It helps you to be a responsible person worthy of trust.

It gives you permission to take charge of your life.

It increases confidence and willpower.

Discipline in Business, Finances and Health

You can tell when discipline is absent in your life, and so can others. You almost always arrive late or cancel at the last minute. People become frustrated and begin without you or start telling you an earlier time, in hopes that you will arrive at the actual time. Sound familiar? If you are constantly feeling there are not enough hours in the day or that others seem to get more done than you, chances are that you need to re-evaluate your time and avoid over-committing. Ephesians 5:11 warns us about this. It says, "Don't waste your time on useless work, mere busywork..." (*MSG*) Later in the same chapter, we are encouraged to make the most of the time we are given. (v.15)

Being disciplined in your personal and professional life can improve your relationships and position you for success. There are enough things going on in our lives and in the lives of those we know and live with. Adding the extra stress that a lack of self- discipline causes can sometimes be unbearable. Your spouse, family and friends become frustrated and even dismayed because as good as your intentions may be, you are just not reliable.

The same is true at work. You may offer your supervisor or co-worker a helping hand, and while they really need your help, they decline your offer because they are not sure whether you will come through. When it's time for your annual review, or possible promotion, these negative characteristics play a role in decision- making. You may be the best person for the job, but your work ethic limits your progress.

Practicing discipline can also play a huge role in your finances. If applied, it will enable you to manage your money more wisely and achieve goals sooner than later. Creating a budget may not seem attractive but applying discipline in your spending is a win-win! For example, putting a certain amount of money in an emergency account will prepare you for the unexpected: a hole in the tire, repairs around the house, an uncovered medical expense, etc. It can facilitate that home or car purchase, long-awaited vacation or paying off a debt.

People who practice this discipline don't wonder or worry about their money because they control its flow rather than being controlled by it. "The wise store up choice food and olive oil, but fools gulp theirs down." (Proverbs 21:20, *NIV*) Don't be like the foolish man. Manage your money well. Don't spend needlessly.

The merchandise at the counter of your favorite store is there for one purpose alone: impulse buying. The items you buy generally aren't on your list. You don't need those things immediately. In fact, you probably don't need them at all; you just want them. After practicing this habit a few days out of the week, you'd be surprised how much it adds up. Unfortunately, the following week, you may be short on a bill. You will have used all your spending money, and you'll be waiting for the next pay day. Then you'll be working for money rather than letting your money work for you.

Once you have learned self-discipline, everything in your life falls in line. This theory holds true for every area including your body because people with self-control maintain their health so that they can accomplish more and enjoy their achievements. There are people who do their morning walk consistently, even if it is raining. Rain is a simple circumstance that can easily be overcome. The person can walk in a mall, exercise in front of their TV or go to a gym if they have a membership. The point is, they must exercise to achieve their health or fitness goals.

The Bible says in 1Thessalonians 4:4, 5: "Learn to appreciate and give dignity to your body, not abusing it, as is so common of those who know nothing of God." (*MSG*) Whether it is your relationships, business practices, finances or health, the disciplines you establish today will determine your success tomorrow. But it takes more than just willpower for lasting self-control. It takes a power greater than yourself: "*For the*

Spirit that God has given us does not make us timid; instead, his Spirit fills us with power, love, and self-control." (2 Timothy 1:7, *GNT*)

The Power in Self-Control

Self-control is a battle between a divided self! One part of us wants to diligently pursue that which we desire, the other part wants to take shortcuts and get the same results.

This poem explains the dilemma well:

Two natures beat within my breast.

The one is foul; the one is blessed.

The one I love, the one I hate.

The one I feed will dominate. ~Anonymous

Despite our greatest effort, there will always be thoughts that conflict with the effort required for discipline. It's like losing weight. The treadmill can become our best friend when it comes to achieving our goals, but the couch and television beckon us to skip a day. We take the day and it becomes two or three days, then a week. The more we put it off, the longer

105

we delay the goal. God's Word teaches us how to deal with this situation. It says that we must "deny ourselves" and "take up our cross daily." The cross represents whatever we must do to achieve the objective. Athletes use great discipline to condition themselves for competition. Their dedication is the same dedication we need to achieve self-control. However, our goal has eternal rewards unlike the temporary rewards athletes receive through medals and ribbons.

Athletes force their bodies to obey their demands so that they can become winners. They continue even when they don't feel like it. Exercising self-control says "no" to sinful desires, even when it hurts. A Christian's level of self-control is not a just-say-no campaign. Our "no" is rooted by faith in the immeasurable power and pleasure of Jesus Christ. In this way our "no" gives Christ all the glory!

According to Galatians 5:22, 23, we have been given certain gifts from God through the Holy Spirit. These gifts are known as *The Fruit of the Spirit:* love, joy peace, patience, kindness, goodness, faithfulness, gentleness, and self-control. (*NIV*) Even the best of us struggle with self-control, and it is difficult to achieve when we try to achieve it through our own strength. Zechariah 4:6 reminds us that is through the precious Holy

Spirit that we gain supernatural strength that can overcome anything. "...

Not by might nor by power, but by My Spirit, says the Lord of hosts."

(*New King James Version*)

If we win by our own strength and might, we get the glory. But when we join our strength with God's strength, He gets the glory and we gain victory! If we win by our own strength and might, we get the glory. But when we join our strength with God's strength, He gets the glory and we gain victory! *So, how do we utilize the fruit of the Spirit to access the gift of self-control?* We stay in God's Word and receive His grace.

The grace that God gives helps us to deny worldly desires in this present age so that we may fight the good fight of faith. God granted the children of Israel the Promised Land. Even though it was a gift, they had to take the land by force. In other words, it wasn't just given to them, they had to fight for it! God has given us the gift of self-control therefore we are empowered to fight the good fight of faith and win in every area of our life.

Overcoming Anger

At least once, over the course of the past week, most of us have gotten angry about something. Whether it was getting cut off in traffic, standing in a long line at the grocery store, or telling the kids for the umpteenth time to clean their rooms, anger has surfaced somewhere along the way. Society is full of angry people who cannot or will not deal with the ugly monster that rises from the back of their minds at will. I know you are thinking, "That is not me! I'm Christ-like and I always ask, 'What would Jesus do?'" We all deal with anger at some point: some more than others.

There exists a passive type of anger. I like to call it "closet anger." Well, the first step to any recovery or deliverance is to admit that you too struggle with anger. You may be one of them. Perhaps when others wave their hands, elevate their voices, turn red-faced or get so pumped that the veins stick out of their necks, you immediately think, "I would never!" The Christian Counselor's Manual (Baker, 359), by Jay E. Adams states, "Anger is a problem for every Christian... ."

Many leading doctors have attributed anger to heart disease and other health issues. Anger can also lead to overeating and excess weight gain.

This is what the Bible says about the issue: *"But now you also, put them all aside: anger, wrath, malice, slander, and abusive speech from your mouth."* (Colossians 3:8, *New American Standard Bible*) Psalm 4:4 also tells us: "Be angry, and yet do not sin; do not let the sun go down on your anger." (*NASB*)

The Bible also refers to *righteous anger* which is "a godly reaction to sin or injustice." That is not the type of anger we are referring to here.

In Genesis 4:6, God asked Cain why he was angry. God never asks questions to gain information; He's God. He already knows. Rather, He asks questions to help us think about the situation from a godly perspective. God had accepted Abel's sacrifice, but He did not accept Cain's. Therefore, Cain felt justified in his anger. But God encouraged him to do what was right despite his anger and jealousy. God also warned Cain that when anger arises, sin enters the door and can easily consume us. Cain ignored God's warning about this destructive emotion. In the end, Cain killed Abel.

It is true that anger is a natural emotion, but it is also true that it can be overcome. Through the indwelling of the Holy Spirit, we can resist the temptation to stay angry. Remember, God never requires us to do what we cannot do without His power. Through the help He provides, we can protect our relationships and bring peace in chaos.

Reputation vs. Integrity

Every person should desire a life full of integrity. This character trait is not just doing what we believe, it is allowing the mind of Christ to direct our words, thoughts and actions. In short, it is a moral code that causes us to act based on belief in God and His Word. Integrity begins as the foundation of every life and it becomes the nails in a sure place. The nails of integrity hold the entire building together despite life's intense pressures. It is a trait of the heart, mind and spirit and one that effective leaders are bound by.

This is an example of a person who lacked integrity. I was invited to emcee a production in California that included award- winning singers and artists. The producer had a great reputation for putting on sell-out shows, and I was flattered by his invitation. Because the company had such a stellar reputation, we agreed that I would pay my travel expenses and later be reimbursed. However, when I arrived, I quickly learned that all the promises had been a lie. The artists were very angry because they had not been paid as agreed. The producer wrote me a check which bounced a couple of times and left me feeling used and disillusioned. That company's reputation had hit the floor for me. But because of my integrity, I tried to keep the event moving forward. To add a sense of calm and remove all the strife that was rising, I began talking, making light jokes, and even preaching at times. The show went on, but lessons had been learned by all.

Healthy, strong reputations are built from a foundation of integrity. The more consistent we are, the higher the degree of integrity we possess and the greater the reputation we earn. The Bible gives great examples of men and women who conducted their lives with integrity. One example is Daniel. He was an upright man and God used him mightily. Daniel held fast to his values and integrity even in the face of slavery and hardship. Because he was consistent in his integrity, the King sought after him to interpret his dreams. *"I have heard of you that the spirit of the gods is in you, and that light and understanding and excellent wisdom are found in you."* (Daniel 5:14, *English Standard Version*)

Because of his reputation, Daniel was able to stand before the king without wavering and speak the truth even though the truth was not what the king wanted to hear.

We are all known by the level of integrity we possess. It is a quality greater than gold and is the basis of trust. Much like a fruit's sweetness is based on the root of a tree, so is integrity based on the condition of our hearts. People are either drawn to us, or just the opposite. When we allow our belief system to be based on God's way, it becomes a solid foundation for which we stand. As a result, people consider us believable and trustworthy.

Humility is usually associated with a person who operates in integrity. A person who is humble is more concerned about doing what is right than they are being right. Such people put lots of effort into acting on good ideas rather than merely having good ideas. They work for the good of the team and are highly comfortable with publicly recognizing the contributions of the team rather than self-elevation.

Don't get me wrong, humility is not weakness. To the contrary, it is power under control! Humble people recognize that they can accomplish so much more by complimenting others rather than criticizing and finding fault. When we choose to live this way, there is no room for pride and arrogance.

It takes courage to stand on godly principles in this world, particularly since so many people are looking out for number one. Oftentimes it means standing alone. Queen Esther was a great example of integrity and humility. Her story is found in the Book of Ester, chapters 1-5. It is a dramatic, inspiring and in some ways a shocking story of the strength of a young woman. Esther was among the women being considered as the next queen. The events recorded read like a newspaper account that might be published in our day and time.

The Bible reports that Esther was a Jew and lived during a time when her people suffered great oppression and racial discrimination. She lived with her cousin, Mordecai, and his family in the country of Persia because Esther's parents died when she was very young. He had been warned by a prophet of God years earlier to flee Persia and return to his homeland to rebuild a temple. Mordecai, along with many other Jews, decided to ignore the warning. They became comfortable in a foreign land, although they were not accepted there.

When Esther was chosen to be among the candidates considered to become queen, Mordecai told her not to reveal that she was a Jew. Esther kept her family's secret. God was working during these circumstances, orchestrating the events in Esther's life. God will do what He wills to carry out His plan and keep His promises to those He loves. You must know that no matter where life leads you, God is always with you working through life's circumstances for your good.

Mordecai worked for the king and was a keeper at the gate controlling who came into the palace. One day as Mordecai was working at the gate, he overheard two of the king's men plotting against him. God had placed Mordecai in the right place at the right time. These two men were angry with King Xerxes, and they were making plans to kill him. Fortunately, Mordecai overheard them and told Esther. She in turn, reported to the King that Mordecai had uncovered the men's plans against the king. The king verified that what he had been told was true and had his two officials put to death.

By reporting this plot, Esther and Mordecai had saved the king's life. You would think their loyalty would put them in good standing with King Xerxes and his court. But the king had another official named Haman whose family had a history showing prejudice toward the Jews. He was promoted to a very high position and the king ordered everyone to bow down to Haman whenever they came in his presence. Mordecai held fast to his belief and would not bow down to anyone except his God. He made this decision knowing that Haman hated the Jews.

When Haman came through the gates, Mordecai would not bow down. The other officials asked him why he would not bow down as the king had ordered. He told them it was because he believed in the only living God, Jehovah. Mordecai's resistance made Haman furious! He eventually learned that Mordecai was a Jew, so out of anger Haman came up with a plan to kill Mordecai and all the Jews in the land. This would be no small feat as the kingdom was far-reaching.

It included many countries populated by hundreds of Jewish families. Haman told King Xerxes his plan. Surprisingly, the king trusted Haman so much that he blindly supported his dastardly plan to kill Mordecai, but he did not fully understand that Haman also planned to perform complete genocide on the Jewish people. In fact, Haman involved the entire government in his plot to eradicate the Jews. The king signed and stamped with approval the letter Haman had prepared communicating his plan. The royal seal moved the plot from a plan to an order that could not be stopped. This was just what Haman needed.

If Mordecai and the other Jews had originally obeyed the prophet's order to leave Persia and return to their homeland, there would not have been any Jews in Persia for Haman to kill. When we follow God's directions, we are under His umbrella of protection. However, when we disobey, it puts us in a place where we are forced to seek God's intervention to avoid the consequences of our disobedience. It's no wonder that all the Jews in Persia were in mourning because the day of their death was quickly approaching.

Just as before, Mordecai sent word to Esther about this plot. He included a copy of the letter decreeing all Jews would die on that day. Mordecai advised Esther to plead for the lives of her people. Terrified and hesitant to go before the king, Esther was not only afraid because she had been dishonest about her nationality, but also because there were very strict laws about visiting the king. No one could just come in the palace to talk with the King on a whim. If the king didn't send for a person, they would have to wait until he pointed his royal scepter giving them permission to speak. This rule was especially enforced for women.

Esther sent word to Mordecai stating it would not be easy for her to take on the task. Mordecai replied reminding Esther she too was a Jew and it would not be long after killing all the other Jews that her life would be in danger too. Esther reconsidered and gathered the courage to break the news to the king. She requested that the Jews to fast for three days on her behalf. After that she would go before King Xerxes.

When three days had passed, Esther dressed in her finest clothing and approached the king's court. Can you imagine the fear running down her spine as she walked toward the throne room? If King Xerxes refused to point his royal scepter at her she would be put to death which ultimately meant all the Jews in the kingdom would die too. As God orchestrated her steps, the king motioned for Esther to come forward. He asked, *"What wilt thou, Queen Esther? And what is thy request? It shall be even given thee to the half of the kingdom"* (Esther 4:3, *KJV*).

The king's response demonstrates the type of favor Esther had with the king. Strategically, she decided to invite King Xerxes and Haman to have dinner with her, and they agreed. Haman was so honored to be invited to dinner by the Queen! He bragged to everyone about it. Haman was an evil man and full of pride. His wife had suggested he build gallows to hang Mordecai, still angry about what happened, he agreed.

Around this time, the king began having trouble sleeping so he asked a servant to bring him the daily chronicles. While reading, he learned that it had been Mordecai who had exposed the plot to kill him and therefore saved his life. The king noticed that Mordecai had not been rewarded for his loyalty and determined he would do so. Isn't it amazing how God works in the middle of a mess? Just when things seem totally out of control and we feel all is lost, God proves once again that He is in control. Just as the King was pondering what to do for Mordecai, Haman entered the courts. Haman was on his way to ask the king for permission to hang Mordecai, but before he could ask, the king asked Haman what he should do to honor the man who saved his life. Thinking King Xerxes was referring to him, Haman began to describe this lavish reward.

This is what Haman said: *"Have your servants get a royal robe you have worn. Have them bring a horse you have ridden on. Have a royal crest placed on its head. Then give the robe and horse to one of your most noble princes. Let the robe be put on the man you want to honor. Let him be led on the horse through the city streets. Let people announce in front of him,*

'This is what is done for the man the king wants to honor!'" (Esther 6:8, 9, *New International Reader's Version*)

Haman was probably picturing himself as the focus of this grand parade. The king liked his idea and commanded Haman to immediately prepare all that he had described stating that Mordecai had been the one to save his life. That statement was a blow to Haman's ego, and it took the wind right out of his sail. It infuriated him, but Haman obeyed. After the big celebration, Haman returned home angry and embarrassed.

When the day had finally come for Haman to attend dinner with the queen and king, Esther finally told the king what she wanted. The Scripture states:

"Then Queen Esther answered, 'King Xerxes, I hope you will show me your favor. I hope you will be pleased to let me live. That's what I want. Please spare my people. That's my appeal to you. My people and I have been sold to be destroyed. We've been sold to be killed and wiped out.'" (Esther 7:3, 4, *NIRV*)

There it was. Esther finally said it! She asked the king to spare her life and the lives of her people. Remember, the king did not know Esther was a Jew. Neither did he know who Esther was referring to when she made him aware that someone was plotting to kill her and her people. The king demanded, "Who is this man? Who is he who dares to do such a thing? Tell me where he is?" Esther informed the king that this man not only hated Jews, but that he also hated her. This further infuriated the king. When she courageously told him that Haman was the man she described, the king decided to hang Haman on the very gallows intended for Mordecai.

Staring Down Your Giants

There may be things in your life that have become increasingly difficult or that cause you fear. It may have been a poor choice, but there are also circumstances that we struggle with that are no fault of our own. It is in unjust times like these that we must realize that God is sovereign, and we never stand alone. Our God is bigger than our circumstances, greater than our trouble, and stronger than our weakest moments. All things work together for our good. This doesn't mean we can just live recklessly and do whatever we want. The Bible is clear that we cannot test or challenge God in this way. We are admonished to follow His instructions which in turn allows us to enjoy the very best that God has for us.

With God on our side, we can find the courage to conquer the issues of our lives. We can stand up to fear even when we feel like quitting. Courage is a character trait of integrity that must be learned and practiced regularly. Winston Churchill said it this way: *"Courage is the first of the human qualities... because it is a quality which guarantees all the others.*

People with courage seem to have the dexterity to keep going despite the challenge's life may bring them. It takes courage to believe that the best is yet to come, and we are better than what we can see today. It is a proven fact that when we exercise the tenacity to believe, we overcome fear. Medically it has been proven that patients who exercise the courage and tenacity to get well, get better more often than not.

Courage is not the absence of fear, because many times courageous people are scared to the core of their being. But they refuse to give fear power over them, so they dig down deep and muster up the strength to go forward. They refuse to say, "I can't do it" and instead say, "I must do it!" This process begins with redefining who we are. We no longer define ourselves by our fears making statements like: "I'm so scared!" "I'm not strong." I'm too shy!" No matter where these thoughts are birthed, once they are conceived in your mind and heart, they begin to control your thoughts and then your life entirely.

Many people think they are broken or that something is wrong with them. Because of this toxic way of thinking, they live within the boundaries of these labels, afraid to venture out. This kind of thinking keeps them in a box unable to move forward. Breaking out of this cycle takes more than just changing your address, moving to a new state or changing your job, although these changes may be beneficial. The most important change is changing your mind! When you change your mind, everything else in your life will follow. Change must be intentional. It becomes a habit. Even if you must face your challenges daily, stare it down and subdue it.

I do not mean to suggest that this is easy to accomplish. I realize that moving toward courage can be scary. It can be like standing before a full auditorium of people to give a speech or looking across the net at the tennis player you have never beaten, or applying for the job you qualify for, but lack the confidence to believe it's yours! Any one of these could be reasons to send you running but fortify your thoughts by avoiding the temptation to overthink things, or worse, talk yourself out of trying at all.

If you find yourself moving backward in your decisions, start working out! Run, join a class, and get moving because building your body in turn builds your mind. Start small and gradually increase your physical strength to increase your mental strength. Become a living testimony of the courage that runs warm through the veins of every believer in Christ. It's your family; it's your heritage! Make it your life!

If we take a walk through the pages of the Bible, we will find others who lived lives laced with outrageous courage. Hebrews 11 gives us a list of men and women who did amazing things by faith with courageous dedication. Too many to name them all, but you walk under the same anointing and call as those listed in the "Hall of Faith" of Hebrews. Each of us has an audience watching us maneuver in and out of life's victories and challenges. You can inspire and strengthen others by the way you approach life.

Women who walk in godly courage depend on God daily, moment by moment. He is their Source, Support and Sustainer. Courageous women trust God and seek His will for their lives. This means they walk in a level of faith that empowers them to move quickly on what they believe God has directed them to do. Women of courage humbly take a stand against injustice wherever they find it because they trust God.

We overcome by the words of their testimonies, too. I read a powerful poem online entitled, "The Strength of a Woman" in the *Saint Paul Almanac* written by New Foundations Writers, (May 7, 2010).

It reads:

The strength of a woman is carrying the

burden of family without expectation

that someone will feel her pain or cry

her tears.

The strength of a woman is the first one

to wake up and the last to go to bed.

The strength of a woman is to pretty and doll

up all the masks she has to wear in order to

survive.

The strength of a woman is crying herself to sleep at night then

embracing you in the morning with a hug and a

smile. The strength of a woman is my mother,

a woman who says she's okay when you can tell she's in pain, a

woman who smiles when the going gets tough and

a woman who finds laughter after crying.

The strength of a woman is to raise a child she does not know. The strength of a woman hears a child's cry and knows exactly what they want.

The strength of a woman is courage and independence. The strength of a woman is doing whatever it takes to survive. The strength of a woman is the backbone

that holds everyone together

. . . behind every strong man there is a strong woman. The strength of a woman is her ability

to hold her tongue when her significant other is

wrong to stop her children from misbehaving with a

look in her eye to pick herself up and dust herself

off

to make her family smile in the midst of a storm to multi-task and adapt to different situations to swallow her pride.

The strength of a woman is her unconditional love for her children and others.

The strength of a woman is to be a peacemaker. The strength of a woman is to be able to

feel things no one else can.

The strength of a woman is to be able.

The strength of a woman is having faith in God, for she knows God is the only one that has her back. Helping others when they are in need, always there to take the lead.

Suffering hard times not for long,

because her will is very strong.

Makes you happy with lots of

jokes, most importantly they are

jokes of hope.

Her colors are beautiful—scarlet

red— lots of blessings upon her

head.

The strength of a woman we'll always know,

because her strength will always show.

---

2 *Founded in 1994, New Foundations is a non-profit organization located on St. Paul's East Side that provides permanent, supportive, affordable housing and comprehensive on-site services for homeless dually diagnosed chemically dependent and mentally ill adults in recovery and their families.*

CHAPTER SEVEN

The Most Fascinating Me I've Never Met

Have you ever wondered what you would be if you didn't worry about failure? Have you ever looked at a faraway star and wondered how high or how far you could go if you loved yourself? The power you can receive by accepting who you are is limitless. This reality of acceptance is seldom traveled because most people have difficulty accepting who they are. Most of our time and energy is spent on trying to get other people to accept us. The Psalmist David finally realized who God created him to be and he wrote it this way:

> *"Oh yes, you shaped me first inside, then out; you formed me in my mother's womb.*
>
> *I thank you, High God—you're breathtaking!*
>
> *Body and soul, I am marvelously made!*
>
> *I worship in adoration—what a creation!*
>
> *You know me inside and out; you know every bone in my body;*
>
> *You know exactly how I was made, bit by bit, how I was sculpted from nothing into something.*
>
> *Like an open book, you watched me grow from conception to birth; all the stages of my life were spread out before you, the*

days of my life all prepared before I'd even lived one day."
(Psalm139:14-16, *MSG*)

This ought to fill your eyes with tears and your heart with joy knowing that a

God so perfect and pure created you with

possibility and promise. Grabbing hold of how truly fascinating you are can be as fleeting as trying to catch lightening bugs in a mason jar.

I wasn't raised in the country, but I loved going to my Uncle John's farm in the summer. It seemed like the longest ride of my life, but once we arrived in Kansas City, Kansas, I couldn't wait to chase bugs that accented the night with their light. They were best seen in the country because there were no streetlights like in the city. Some areas of the country had lots of trees causing the night to appear as dark as a hundred midnights. But these small, insignificant bugs could light up a dark spot like nothing else could. They created a glow that made the night a fascinating mystery in the mind of a child.

This lightening bug's impact in darkness can be likened to the light God has place on the inside of you! It is a fascinating light which you may have yet to discover. Have you looked inward? Have you dug deep into the corners of your own soul? Isn't it strange how some people waste years trying to become what others say we *should* be instead of investing life in becoming the fascinating person we were created to be? You were designed with precision and care, with the loving touch of our Father, God. The intricacy of your internal design impacts your external appearance and impact. The light within you has the capacity to illuminate the purposeful destiny of your life.

Adopting Someone Else's Light

When I consider how we sometimes waste time trying to live out someone else's destiny, I am reminded of the time King Saul sent David into battle wearing the king's armor. David was a boy when King Saul sought men to be warriors in battle. Confident that he could do the job, David volunteered. Since he was young and likely smaller than the average man, King Saul gave David his personal armor to protect him. However, when David entered battle, he realized the armor was too cumbersome to fight effectively, so he removed the king's armor and fought successfully.

Like David, you have been blessed with your own unique way of bringing light into darkness. Trying to live under the pretense of someone else's light won't get the job done. Perhaps you haven't embraced the free-spirited, confident, and unique person God has made you to be the you

129

that you haven't met yet. The person you were truly meant to be possesses a special quality that fills your soul with vivacious passion! This passion reveals to the world that you are one of a kind, a designer's original.

Job said in essence that God does great things beyond our understanding. *"He says to the snow, 'Fall on the earth,' and to the rain shower, 'Be a mighty downpour.'"* (Job 37:6, *NIV*) God even commands the elements to do what they were created to do! He desires the same thing for you. If this applies to you, stop trying to mimic others and set that woman you've never met free! Some people never release that person inside and thus settle for less, many times without knowing it. Many come to the misguided conclusion that whatever they can get is better than nothing at all. The problem with that mentality is that better than nothing is really nothing in disguise.

Whenever you gain something that is neither satisfying nor enjoyable, it is like having nothing at all. If you have to talk yourself into being nice, passionate, or excited, you aren't really enjoying life and its many events. That means you've settled for less. When you think of a relationship, business or venture you're involved in and all you can do is count the time and energy you put into it, there is no real appreciation or gratification from your efforts. You have settled. When you spend more time complaining about the cost instead of enjoying the journey, you have settled indeed. If this describes certain aspects of your life, it is time to dig deep until you find the amazing person God has created you to be.

Friendship with oneself is all important, because without it one cannot be friends with anyone else in the world.

~ Eleanor Roosevelt

It is amazing the number of people who complain about their lives, believing there is no way they can find happiness with what they have right now. They concern themselves with who has the most toys and they equate happiness to being rich with an abundance of friends, being famous and or possessing wealth.

Happiness begins internally before external gain is added. If there is breath and life in your body, it is not too late to begin building inner happiness, joy, and peace.

Speak Life into Your Situation

The Bibles teaches that the power of life and death is in our tongue! In other words, what you say matters! Your words form your spiritual world and it becomes the foundation of your physical life. You must intentionally say what you want and stop saying what you hate about your life. The Bible says call things that are not as though they were! So, speak the changes you want to see.

This process moves from the words you speak to aligning your actions with the same. This is the only way to manifest the life you want in the physical world. When you pray, don't concern yourself with what others have acquired or compare yourself to them. Don't even waste your time coveting anything they have. God has a reservoir of blessings set aside just for you! Therefore, develop a clear vision of where you want to go and what you want to accomplish.

Begin by seeking God for His plan for your life. Sometimes your purpose can be revealed in doing the things you love. In fact, try doing at least one thing you enjoy every day. It doesn't have to be big or require money. If you think about it, there are many things that can bring you fulfillment in a typical day. For example, watching the sun rise or set, thumbing through

132

those magazines that are collecting dust, or talking to a family member or friend.

As you intentionally begin speaking God's best into your life and nurturing a positive attitude, be sure you surround yourself with people of the same mindset. Toxic people can poison your efforts. Maybe you have been associating with people who complain because you have been a complainer as well. If that is the case, begin finding good things to say. Try to see the good in every situation, or at least declare that although things may be tough, you will overcome. These small steps will bring more fulfillment into your life. Your positive approach may even rub off on others who complain or possess negative energy.

You can also contribute to the happiness of others by volunteering at your church, in your community or with a non- profit organization. These efforts will pull your focus away from you and put the needs of others first. Small acts of kindness go a long way, and thcy will bring you great joy and fulfillment as well. Limit your exposure to negative influences such as television, social media, gossiping and the like. These actions hinder your happiness. Look for and appreciate the small things; be positive, choose to be happy and decide to love your life!

CHAPTER EIGHT

Confidently Me

"She is clothed with strength and dignity, and she laughs without fear of the future." (Proverbs 31:25, *NLT*)

God created women to be confident, secure, and satisfied. Over the centuries, we have digressed from the former role Eve was given, along with Adam, to rule, have dominion, and create. Eve supported Adam as a co-creator and ruler over the Garden of Eden. She was clearly not afraid to speak or use her authority as demonstrated in the interaction with the serpent, and the decision she made that changed the course of life for generations.

Since that time, women have been chasing their value and authority in the world and within their own lives. Although confidence can be seen in the way women conduct themselves, it really has very little to do with what is going on externally. Confidence starts on the inside which should be our focus as we expand in this area. Psalm 31 outlines many characteristics of a virtuous woman some of which we will focus on in this chapter.

To begin, let's look at a few traits. The Message translation reads: *"She's up before dawn preparing breakfast for her family and organizing her day"* (v. 15). *"First thing in the morning, she dresses for work, rolls up her sleeves, eager to get started. She senses the work of her work and is in no hurry to call it quits for the day" (vv.17, 18). From this Scripture we gather that to be successful, women must rise early to be organized, prepared for the day, and in doing so committed to meet the goals she has established for each day.*

Enhance Inner Beauty

Have you ever walked by a car window and felt an irresistible urge to check out your reflection? Or maybe you have felt self- conscious because of an unwanted blemish on your face. If so, you are aware of one of the universal truths of being a woman: no matter how old we are, our appearance matters, sometimes too much. "Charm can mislead, and beauty soon fades. The woman to be admired and praised is the woman who lives in the Fear- of-God" (v. 30). This Scripture reminds us that a virtuous woman should take great care in preserving her appearance.

Another universal truth, however, is that physical beauty will ultimately fade. Over the course of our lifetime, we will gain and lose weight, develop wrinkles, and lose hair. However, we learn in Psalm 31 that a truly beautiful woman does not have to use her body to get attention, it is her inner spirit that should be given the greatest focus as it relates to self-care. Although physical beauty is an asset and does draw attention, internal beauty is most valuable, and it never withers nor fades.

This woman cares for her body and prepares healthy food for herself and her family if she has one. She takes time to exercise to keep her body under control, because she has learned self- control. The confident woman is eager to lend a hand wherever it is needed. She is always cognizant to serve her husband, family, friends, and community. She is kind and possesses a gentle spirit.

It is a woman's relationship with God that makes a woman attractive, strong, and confident. Her character is defined by how she continues to unfold in her walk with Him. The aforementioned Scripture demonstrates that a virtuous woman reverences and respects God. This should be evident in every aspect of her life! There is nothing more attractive and admirable than a woman who is

unshakeable because her confidence is not tied to her lips, tips, or hips. Instead, it oozes from the depths of her soul, and her love for Almighty God. The way she carries herself inspires others to become better. The joy of the Lord is the source of her very existence! And her strength lies in the confidence that God is ever-present and will never leave her.

Women who exude confidence also inspire and motivate the men in their lives. Part of the inspiration derives from the fact that the virtuous woman is not desperate for a man or his attention. A confident woman compliments a man's style and boosts his assuredness. This is a major attribute in the male-female dynamic. *"Her husband can trust her, and she will greatly enrich his life. She brings him good, not harm, all the days of her life."* (vv. 11 , 12 , *N L T*) A trustworthy person operates in the highest integrity, morals and values. This characteristic is one that we must all seek to emulate. Trust is the cousin of respect. Respect is what most men yearn for and seek in their relationships with

others, especially women.

137

If a woman is married, she must maintain a high level of respect for her husband. The virtuous woman does her husband well all the days of his life. Her husband puts his utmost trust in her because she is trustworthy. On the other hand, if you are single, understand that a woman of virtue carries herself in such a way that suitors are immediately drawn to her, and her demeanor demands

respect.

When our focus is on getting attention or competing with others, we harm the people around us. Motives become twisted when this occurs which causes a woman to begin looking to men as a source to feel better about themselves or take care of them, whereas building a relationship should be the focus. Rather than considering women as potential friends, she begins looking at them as competitors. The dreadful end is that she is never able to engage in the relationships she wants and needs. Instead, she ends up driving people away in her pursuit for attention.

We don't have to belittle ourselves by seeking attention and approval. Placing our focus on building valuable relationships – male and female – and building our internal strengths should be our focus. Only then can we end the deep-seated cravings for attention and competition. Our goal should be to live for God's approval. Each of us has a God-designed purpose to enrich the lives of others.

Character Attributes of the Virtuous and Confident Woman

Confident women are known for their love and their ability to shift the center of their world from themselves to God. When the focus is on God and not ourselves, our God-given abilities kick in to care about other people, and we find ourselves doing things that we wouldn't have normally done on our own. The Bible says this about the Proverbs 31 woman: *"She extends a helping hand to the poor and opens her arms to the needy."* (v. 20, *NLT*) She didn't wait for people to ask for help. She reached out to the poor, even if it meant putting their needs before her own. Likewise, with wide open arms, we should also reach out to help, touch and support others who may have never experienced this kind of agape love. We can accomplish great things when we are confident and close to God.

To become a confident woman, we must do the spiritual work! Faith is the basis for all she does, and it shines like a beacon of light! The virtuous woman described in the Bible was full of faith. Therefore, before we attempt to gain any other trait, we must first gain great faith. This is attained by serving God with all our heart, mind and soul. We must constantly seek His will when making decisions and willingly follow His lead.

The Message Bible tells us that a virtuous woman manages her life, business, and finances successfully: *"She looks over a field and buys it, then, with money she's put aside, plants a garden."* (v. 16) She is a true entrepreneur, and researches investments for the greatest possible returns. When she finds land that is profitable, she buys it. In this day and age, it really doesn't matter whether it is land, stocks, savings, bonds, or a simple checking account, we must plan wisely and in advance.

Another trait worth emulating from the virtuous woman is being purposeful and savvy. The example we read about in Proverbs 31 acquired skill in what was needed in her time. She didn't wait for things to come to her; she went out of her way to seize every opportunity. She kept her house tidy and in order, and did not allow important things to go undone. The Scriptures attest to her tenacious character: *"She is skilled in the crafts of home and hearth, diligent in homemaking."* (v. 18, *MSG*) From this excerpt of the virtuous woman, we gather that this woman used her learned abilities to make her home attractive and clean while shopping in places that did not break her budget.

We learn more about this woman's business savvy in verses 4 and 5: *"She shops around for the best yarns and cottons, and enjoys knitting and sewing. She's like a trading ship that sails to faraway places and brings back exotic surprises."*

(*MSG*) This girl was on top of her game! She knew her business and wasn't afraid to go far and wide to accomplish her goals. She was a wise and sharp shopper and always worked for the good of her family. She was frugal and learned what was needed to be a successful entrepreneur.

A confident woman nurtures. She teaches her children the ways of the Lord and demonstrates the love of Christ even when she disciplines them with care and wisdom. *"When she speaks she has something worthwhile to say, and she always says it kindly. She keeps an eye on everyone in her household and keeps them all busy and productive"* (vv. 25, 26, *MSG*)

A virtuous and confident woman is on top of her finances. She spends her money wisely being careful to purchase quality items needed by her family. This type of woman has an entrepreneurial spirit and uses godly wisdom to prepare for the future. She has learned from God's Word that it is He who gives us the power to gain wealth. She willingly engages in education and training to improve her city and state. This woman works with her hands to create an inviting atmosphere of warmth, peace and love for her family, friends and guests. Her confident use of hospitality ministers to everyone around her and visitors love coming to her home and have a hard time leaving.

She uses her time wisely and diligently to complete her daily tasks. She plans ahead and stores what she needs during prosperous times to cover herself (and her family) when times become lean. She also understands the value of time and uses it wisely by not spending time dwelling on things from the past.

This confident woman knows her worth and beauty. She is not stuck on superficial things but lives by an inner code of beauty that can only come from her time in God's presence. She uses her creativity and sense of style to create beauty in and around her life, as well as for others.

You may be asking, *"How can I laugh when the bills are due, and I don't have enough money to make ends meet?"* It is because you know in Whom you trust, and this is another opportunity for God to show himself strong on your behalf. You may not be sure how things are going to work out but have the boldest of confidence in your Lord and Savior Jesus Christ because in the same way He takes care of the sparrows, He takes care of you. Your complete confidence must be in Him.

It Is Your Time to Shine

God has given us the example of the virtuous woman as a guide. It is not to discourage us or disqualify us, rather it is to help us evaluate our lives for improvement in the various capacities in which we operate. You are predestined for greatness and confidence is a valuable component to you reaching your purpose. Studying the life of the virtuous woman will help you grow to new heights which is also my prayer for you. The Bible indicates that she wore purple which is a royal color that symbolizes wealth.

A new level of confidence is waiting for you. Do not sit there waiting for something to happen. Believe by faith that God is ordering your steps. The woman in Proverbs accepted that she was a daughter of the One True King and she was not embarrassed by it. In fact, it increased her confidence. Would the daughter of a king, president or ruler have any need to feel less than or live in fear and intimidation? Of course not! Neither do you. You share the same lineage as this woman.

It's not always about having a lot of money to buy the finest things, rather it is the state of your heart and mind. That will get you where money can't take you.

This woman was so confident that she laughed in the face of fear. Proverbs 31:22, 25 says, "...She dresses in fine linen and purple gowns. She is clothed with strength and dignity, and she laughs without fear of the future." (*NLT*)

You may be asking, *"How can I laugh when the bills are due, and I don't have enough money to make ends meet?"* It is because you know in Whom you trust, and this is another opportunity for God to show himself strong on your behalf. You may not be sure how things are going to work out but have the boldest of confidence in your Lord and Savior Jesus Christ because in the same way He takes care of the sparrows, He takes care of you. Your complete confidence must be in Him.

Have you ever met someone, and it seemed as if every word that came out of their mouth was as sweet as honey? It just encouraged you to take on the world and gave you life. This is the type of woman God wants you to be. He wants us to inspire other women and to empower them. But not just them, He wants us to be an encourager for all the people you encounter. It's time to start building each other up. So, find a mentor with these qualities who will help you become accountable to yourself and to your destiny.

I really love the woman described in Proverbs 31. As I envisioned organizing my life patterned by her example, I thought that I could be as amazing as she was. After giving prolonged thought to this incredible model of a Christian woman, I became intimidated by her. One thing I learned in dissecting her qualities and pulling them into the 21st century is that she could be any woman living anywhere in the world, not just a married woman. That ah-ha moment made me realize that I didn't have to become exactly who she was, trait upon trait. That would be impossible anyway.

God wants us to extract the concept of being a virtuous woman in this day. We don't need to get stuck on every single detail about the biblical character in Proverbs. We certainly don't need servants or to spin wool and make clothing.

God isn't expecting perfection in us; there is only One who is perfect. However, He is expecting that we grow into the person He has called us to be as we reach toward destiny. Within, we possess all that we need to be the mother, sister, wife, friend, entrepreneur, and virtuous woman He has called and anointed us to be. This model of the virtuous woman gives us the courage to be all that we can be, for Christ's sake.

As women, let us commit to go the extra mile to elevate our faith, elevate our thinking and elevate our spirit to shine brightly in this world in which we live. It may require that we wake up earlier, adjust our attitudes, check our motives, or increase our faith, but it will be well-worth our while.

CHAPTER NINE

Mentors and Other Needful Things

"Therefore encourage one another and build each other up. ..."
(1Thessalonians. 5:11, *NIV*   )

The Bible shares a wonderful story of how a special bond was formed between two women, Ruth, and Naomi, who came together out of sorrow and grief due to the deaths of their husbands. Ruth, who was married to one of Naomi's sons, helped Naomi to overcome the loss of her husband and her two sons. Although Ruth was a young woman, she remained with her mother-in-law, and was equipped by God to help Naomi reach her destiny.

There will be times in our lives when we will need someone to guide us onto the path prescribed for us. These blessed people come along offering us words of encouragement at times, while sometimes having to convict us with words of truth, especially when we have little capacity to do this for ourselves. Often, these are God-ordained connections built out of love to help us develop spiritually. We can each be that person who shares the

147

assurance of the hope we always have in the Lord Jesus Christ. In our pursuit to matter and make a difference, we can each be a loving, supportive member of a beautiful, mentoring relationship.

The Exchange

When we consider the mentoring relationship between Naomi and Ruth, it could easily be assumed that the elder woman, Naomi, would be the mentor, guiding and training the younger woman. But if you look a little deeper at what is said in Scripture, you will conclude that their relationship was so much more than a mother/ daughter-like relationship. Scripture draws a beautiful picture of two women who exchanged what they had to benefit the other. It was a covenant − sacred, ordained and anointed by the Father. What is clear is that the relationship between these two women had its basis in their mutual commitment to God. They helped each other heal from their pain and grief by encouraging each other through their faith in God.

These women were not only connected by marriage, but they were also connected by choice. Yes, their relationship was God- ordained, but they were not without a choice. Ruth could have gone back to her homeland, like Orpah (Naomi's other daughter- in-law), had done, or she could have set out on a journey alone. Ruth and Naomi teach us that lasting, beneficial relationships are all centered on God. Regardless of whether it is a marriage relationship, a sacred friendship, or a mentorship, it will become foundational to our lives and growth when God is at the center.

These words found in *30 Essential Lessons from Women of the Bible,* author Freeman-Smith, further emphasize this point:

> (Worthy Media, 2012).*"God does not intend that you experience mediocre relationships. He created you for far greater things. Building lasting relationships requires compassion, wisdom, empathy, kindness, courtesy, perseverance, and forgiveness. If it sounds like a lot of work, it is – which is perfectly fine with God. Why? Because He knows you are capable of doing that work and because He knows that the fruits of your labors will enrich the lives of your loved ones and the lives of generations unborn."*

I cannot stress enough the importance of connecting with a mentor or joining a group where mentoring takes place. Regardless of how people may view mentoring, it is a biblical concept. Although the word "mentor" is never used in the Bible, the principles of mentoring are found throughout the Scriptures. There are numerous examples of mentoring relationships. Sometimes mentoring happened on a one-on-one basis, and in other cases mentoring took place within small groups. Jesus mentored twelve, sometimes three, and on rare occasions, one. Jesus, our perfect example, modeled mentoring in many of His interactions with others. It was how He passed His passion to His disciples, and it is how we can pass ours to others.

The story of Naomi and Ruth isn't necessarily meant to show that young adults desire relationships of this nature. However, emerging generations recognize almost naturally that they have a lot to learn, and the Bible affirms a relationship model of mentoring that can be used to meet that need.

Accessibility, Freedom and Honesty

A successful mentoring relationship focuses on the progress, growth, and success of the mentee. The guidance of the mentor is best served when it addresses the mentee's present life needs. A keen mentor will listen and learn, asking the mentee questions to discover where the mentee would like to go and what he or she wants to learn. After making this type of discovery, the mentor serves as a guide toward the desired end.

The misconception that the mentor must be a scholar spewing out an abundance of knowledge on any given subject or having a thorough knowledge of the Bible discourages many from stepping up to mentor young people seeking direction for their lives. When we consider the term "guide," what we discover is that a guide's purpose is to assist anyone traveling the path he or she has already traveled, offering information about his or her own travels and warning the mentee of impending danger. A guide also assists when things have gone wrong.

The goal of the Christian mentor is to change lives through the application of biblical truths. The role of the mentee should be to actively listen and receive guidance that will enable him or her to discover the destiny and purpose of his or her life. Therefore, in- depth discussions are necessary. Feel free to ask questions so that you may receive helpful information. This relationship is effective when it is reciprocal, with effective communication flowing between both parties. Authentic mentorship happens when both parties share real-life experiences, not just successes, though they are equally important. The good, the bad, and the ugly must be discussed to expose brokenness and promote healing.

Mentees yearn for honesty from a mentor, looking for those who are willing to share their mistakes and path to recovery. When a mentor is this transparent, it increases the faith, hope and strength of the mentee. A mentee must be careful not to approach the relationship with unrealistic expectations. The mentor should not be expected to meet the mentee's personal needs, and he or she may not be able to meet *all* the mentee's mentoring needs. These types of expectations will put a strain on the relationship and may cause it to end prematurely.

When you find the group or person you would like to work with, be sure you have done your homework by predetermining what you want to accomplish through this relationship. Ensure that your interactions are intentional and valuable, or both of you will lose interest. Finally, it is recommended that both parties establish rules of confidentiality to support mutual trust. If trust is lost, it is almost impossible to reclaim.

Titus 2:3-5 gives us the groundwork for intentionally developing friendships among women from different generations. It talks about women investing in the lives of one another by giving encouragement and guidance, listening and sharing and enjoying love and laughing with one another. The goal is to form strong bonds and lasting relationships between women who are willing to be a source of support, strength, and growth to other women.

A circle of support is vital for your continued growth and healing. One thing I have learned over the thirty-plus years in my career is that many of my accomplishments and the good things I have experienced were rarely accomplished alone. Most of my successes were securely connected to getting the right advice and backing from the right person or people.

Throughout our lives, we have had the benefit of mentors, even when we didn't realize it. For many of us, our mentors were our parents, grandparents, and other family members, not to mention peers, teachers and pastors. Every great craftsman learned his or her craft from a leader in the industry. Having the right mentor means connecting to someone who has accomplished what you're trying to accomplish. He or she has walked that path and knows the sacrifices that must be made and the pitfalls that must be avoided to succeed.

Many people look for mentors who have connections for networking purposes.

Networking is beneficial, but these relationships are so much more than that. Mentors can teach skills and give sound advice for a specific field, and they have the potential to boost the self-esteem of their mentees like no other person can.

A mentor has been given the power to speak into the mentee's life, preparing the mentee to embrace his or her destiny. As women, we are often our worst enemies. We criticize ourselves beyond what others think about us, dragging childhood issues into our adult lives and disqualifying ourselves before trying. In contrast, men tend to feel positive about accomplishing a task until they are told they can't or that they are not doing a good job. On the other hand, women tend to think they can't until someone tells them they can, or until they are told they are doing a good job. Women clearly have a sense of subservience that has been deeply planted into our minds from centuries of set beliefs that have been hard to change.

Choosing the Best Candidate

Women have had great success in working their way out from under centuries of believing this way. Changing this type of belief becomes easier when the guidance of a trusted mentor is involved. This valuable partnership could mean empowering a woman to overcome internal and external factors that have been hindering her progress. "So," you may ask, "how do I find a good mentor?" I'm so glad you asked. Finding a mentor begins with you. Start thinking of people you admire for their achievements, industry experience or ability to work well with others.

Your mentor should be someone who shares your professional, personal and faith outlook on life. If that person has already accomplished the goals you hope to attain, that's even better! Before you ask someone to mentor you, invite him or her for coffee or lunch and pick their brain about their experiences to get the best idea of how your relationship with them will work.

Take your time. You want your mentor to be supportive, communicative, and inspiring. He or she must feel that your needs are important. Get to know the person well; build a relationship with them so that you are comfortable with sharing your struggles and issues with them. If you don't know someone offhand, look for someone connected to the community or involved in your church or organization. Remember, a mentor isn't someone who tells you what to do; it is someone who encourages you to seek and find your own answers.

Your job as a mentee is to be open to new ideas, act on the guidance given, and be prepared to adapt and change. Once you determine whether your mentor is for professional or spiritual guidance or both, I recommend creating an agreement or contract for the length of time you will invest in your meetings, creating a schedule that works for both of you. Working with a mentor can cause some uneasiness at times because he or she will try to pull you out of your comfort zone so that you can experience greater success. Accept the challenge; you will be better because of it.

One More Bit of Advice

My editor is screaming right about now because I just feel the need to add this tidbit of information. It's not on topic at all, but I believe it is important to add. So, pardon me for taking this short rabbit trail, but I pray this information will be a blessing to you.

While mentoring is important to your success, so is proper management of your money. Positioning oneself to be secure in life and death should be at the core of every Christian's thoughts, desires, and plans. The importance of knowing your financial reality must become a key part of your plans for security – for you and your family. Managing your finances includes mapping out a strategy that will increase your streams of income. To be successful, you must continuously seek knowledge and alliances that promote the practice of wise money management. In fact, it is not a bad idea to have a financial mentor to help you in this area.

Taking a hard look at your finances can be like watching the latest horror movie. Although you may be scared out of your wits, you continue to look, peeking through your fingers while covering your eyes, hoping to miss the goriest parts. It may sound funny, but this is how many of us approach our financial habits, preferring not to really look at our actions and the results of them. The reality is, you must open your eyes, even if you dislike the current picture. Like anything else, it can change.

As the daughters of God, we should be living a blessed life, lacking nothing. God's Word tells us so. However, the promises in the Bible are always associated with a premise. God says you can have what He promises if you do what He says! Many have practiced good habits as it pertains to giving to the work of the Lord through tithes and offerings. This is a necessary thing. However, being a good steward also means utilizing and managing all resources God provides for His glory and for the betterment of His creation. The

Deuteronomy 28:1-6 puts it this way:

Carefully obey the Lord your God, and faithfully follow all his commands that I'm giving you today. If you do, the Lord your God will place you high above all the other nations in the world. These are all the blessings

that will come to you and stay close to you because you OBEY the LORD your God:

You will be blessed in the city and blessed the country.

You will be blessed. You will have children. Your land will have crops. Your animals will have offspring. Your cattle will have calves, and your flocks will have lambs and kids.

The gain you harvest and the bread you bake will be blessed. You will be blessed when you come and blessed when you go. (*God's Word Translation*)

God is faithful to His promises to us when we are faithful to His premises. In nature, we plant seeds to grow a flower, tree, fruit, or vegetable. Without planting the seed, there is no return. The same is true in God's kingdom of financial harvest. God promises blessings upon our lives, our family, and our world. However, these promises hinge on the premise of our obedience. There are natural laws in place on Earth to produce a great harvest. In the same way, there are spiritual laws for blessings that will produce abundance in our lives.

Following God's premises holds true for dying, as well. If you desire to go to Heaven and be with the Lord when you die, there are principles that must be followed. Intentionally seeking God and living according to His instructions, will bring you to a glorious eternal life in Heaven.

The woman who comes to realize this truth will reap abundance. Few people stumble into abundance; there are certain practices that lead to it becoming a reality. Abundance can only be achieved through intentional living, purposeful spending and wise decisions. This is God's desire for each of us: *Dear friend, I'm praying that all is well with you and that you enjoy good health in the same way that you prosper spiritually.* (3 John 1:2, *Common English Bible*)

Above everything, God desires prosperity and health for each of us. The measurement of this desire is that you prosper spiritually. Since God desires this for us, why don't we have it? Could it be that we have not done the spiritual work to prosper and to have good health? To receive anything from God, you must first believe that you can possess it. So many people want instant gratification from God. They want instant answers to their prayers, instant

prosperity for their needs, and instant health.

Of course, it is possible for God to fulfill our desires instantly, but He uses the power of process to bring us closer to Him. When you realize that staying in prayerful contact with God is a condition of receiving His promises, that knowledge will liberate you. He gives us permission to remind Him of His promises. So, when you pray, rather than using your word, use God's Word. Say it back to Him because all His promises are "Yes" in Jesus Christ. Ask Him to show you and lead you into prosperity and health. But you must be willing to do it HIS way. We do not serve an impotent God, or a God of lack. He is a God of abundance who holds the worlds in His hands. All things are possible with God, and nothing is impossible for those who believe.

CHAPTER TEN
Fear: The Enemy
in Me

Fear, in and of itself, has a purpose. When you are in a scary situation, it's important that you know what you are feeling and why! If your life is threatened, your feelings of fear are meant to keep you safe. Fear sends adrenaline shooting through your veins, causing you to react. Understanding fear when it comes to relationships, however, can sometimes be hard to identify because you're not in fear for your life. Although you cannot pinpoint the threat, it is very real. This anxiety stems from a fear of establishing intimate relationships that will keep you closely connected to other people. It can be referred to as the "fear of intimacy," and can manifest in different ways. Let's discuss a few of them.

Fear of Being Abandoned

Loving relationships involve risks. Both parties must be willing to be vulnerable to develop a committed relationship. From the moment you commit to being in a loving relationship with someone, you live with the risk of being left alone. That daily struggle can be very scary. Dealing with the thought of opening your heart and allowing someone in only to have him or her leave you can create a heavy weight of anxiety. The fear of heartbreak becomes especially terrifying if you have been waiting a while for the "real deal:" the man or woman of your dreams!

Any fear that causes you not to enjoy life and live it to the fullest is not from God. It is from the enemy, Satan, according to 2 Timothy 1:7. Fear is the king of all the spirits that try to hold us back. It is the spirit he uses to distract and destroy the lives of God's people. Fear can be tormenting and can keep you from enjoying life and important relationships.

Fear of Being Smothered

One thing we all can admit is that being single comes with a lot of freedom. When a person is single, he or she decides what to do or not do with his or her time. Choices and priorities are set unilaterally. The idea of a close, committed relationship presents challenges and problems when it comes to relinquishing that sense of freedom. Even though you may want a genuine, lasting, and loving relationship, part of you may be afraid that having this relationship is going to take away your freedom. Some counselors call this "the common other-half mentality," which leads to fear about getting into a committed relationship. This theory indicates that individuals feel incomplete until they find a partner, but they feel like they must compromise a great deal to gain one. The compromise could include the potential loss of individuality, autonomy, and personal space.

Although we, as individuals, may want to be in a committed relationship, we are also equally afraid of being left *and* of losing ourselves. In this case, our only choice is to free ourselves from the fear that is keeping love at a distance. It's no wonder why finding a great partner and creating a healthy relationship feels like a shot in the dark. Once you confront and get rid of these fears, the chains that have held you back come crashing down, and their effects are no longer running your life. Only then will you be open to love flowing into your life so abundantly that you won't want it to stop.

Fear of Rejection

Being told not to fear is easier said than done. Fear has a way of creeping into the smallest situation, even when you feel you have closed all your vulnerable openings. It is a fight you must be up for to maintain your stance and succeed. Oftentimes the fear of rejection can come in so quietly that it is unnoticed and becomes a constant companion and source of oppression in our lives. But we must be vigilant when it comes to recognizing fear and its effects on our lives so that we can take the necessary steps to be free from it. I want to introduce you to "Marilyn."

On the surface, Marilyn is a beautiful, outgoing, intelligent, and athletic young woman. She has advanced degrees, as well as a counseling license. I was drawn to her because of her sincere desire to fit in and connect with a passionate group. We began to work together. As we talked and became more acquainted, I found that her conversation was laced with the fear of being rejected. She explained that she wanted to be more closely involved with other people, but she was convinced that most people wouldn't accept her. According to her, "they never have."

Marilyn continued to explain that her decisions were usually based on those feelings. When we were alone and able to talk at length, I inquired about her previous relationships. Marilyn told me she had been in several serious relationships, but because of her fear, she ended the relationships because she feared being abandoned and rejected by them, just as she had been by her parents. I asked Marilyn if we could talk further about this issue, find the cause, and destroy it at the root. She was more than willing to do so.

At our next meeting, Marilyn described herself as someone who had few original thoughts. Because she didn't want people to reject her, she usually waited for others to suggest things and then jumped onboard with their ideas. She considered herself a "people watcher," but her objective was not to learn from them, but to copy their behaviors, conversations, and styles. She believed if she acclimated to the way other people thought and acted it would be easier to fit in and be accepted.

When Marilyn was five years old, her parents decided to divorce and sent her to live with her grandparents. She overheard them yelling at each other about which of them should be responsible for her. The final analysis was that neither of her parents *wanted* her! To her young mind, that meant she didn't matter. It was the beginning of Marilyn's struggle with feelings of rejection.

Although her grandparents had a stable home, she never felt "good enough." They withheld love when she misbehaved and compared her to others so harshly that she began to mimic those people to gain her grandparent's acceptance. Now, there is nothing wrong with reflecting examples of good behavior. All of us do this from time to time, but there is a big difference in mirroring the behaviors of others out of the fear of rejection. It is important that we never lose ourselves.

While struggling for acceptance as a young girl, Marilyn lost all sense of identity. Her personal identity had to be restored so that she would be able to live in a healthy emotional state of mind. Marilyn realized that her fear of rejection made her "needy," and it likely contributed to the demise of her relationships. Marilyn needed people to make her "feel" happy. She craved attention and found it extremely difficult to say no!

When people sense that you are needy and seek constant approval, they will either manipulate you for their own purposes, or they will take you for granted.

Either way you lose. You matter too much to God to ever allow that to happen! People are naturally drawn to and want to associate with those who are confident. They want to be with people who value their own worth and know they matter. They are rarely manipulated or taken for granted because they walk in the confidence of their self-worth. That should be our goal.

Marilyn admitted living most of her life in extreme dissatisfaction with almost everything she had accomplished. She explained that even though she was well-educated and had multiple degrees, she still did not feel significant. In other words, she did not feel she mattered. She admitted she had never been truly happy. These feelings of inadequacy all stemmed from the rejection she experienced as a 5-year-old little girl.

Self-Analysis of the Fear Factor

Since Marilyn was able to pinpoint when the root of rejection began, we were able to create steps toward healing. The first step was to figure out what she really wanted. If you suffer from a fear of rejection, I want you to ask yourself what you want for *your* life. Then explore the reasons why. Be sure that your reasons have nothing to do with what others think or want for you. The reasons must be legitimate so that you may build a solid future. Part of your *why* should also involve areas of your life that require healing. Once you have found the *why*, next determine how you will benefit from what you want, and how it will impact your future. What are you looking forward to doing or becoming? What could possibly happen if you fail to heal? Take time to make your answers meaningful and write them down.

The next step is to gain clear vision. This means looking at what it is exactly that you fear! If this is not known, there are a few questions you can ask yourself. For example: *"What type of rejection am I afraid of?"* *"Whose rejection do I fear the most?"* *"How do I behave when I fear being rejected"* *"How does this behavior hinder me?"* *"How is it hurting me?"* If it is not a fear of rejection that you struggle with, identify the root of any fears you may have.

After you have identified your fear and the negative behaviors associated with it, establish positive responses to any negativity that exists within. Take time to name potential obstacles standing in the way of your freedom. Are they real or imagined? What steps can you take to overcome these obstacles, both real and imagined? Give yourself time to think through all obstacles that you might need to work through to fully embrace your newly- found freedom. Then begin working on them just one at a time.

Remember, lasting change is not a microwave process. Commit to ongoing, daily self-improvement. These steps are the bricks and mortar of pulling your life together and building your self-esteem over time. The passing of time should help you build new social skills. We live in a social world and interact with others daily. During some of these interactions, you may be criticized, judged, and rejected. It is unavoidable; all of us must prepare for these encounters. Even though you can't control what other people think or do, you can minimize the impact rejection has on you by developing your social skills and your ability to assert yourself when required. The more you work through this process, the more confidence you will have within, giving you the ability to be free of the fear of rejection and live as an overcomer.

Godly Fear

Although there is such a thing as sinful (or evil) fear, there is also godly (or reverent) fear. Godly fear is reverential respect for our salvation through Jesus Christ and all that He is developing us to be. We show reverence and godly fear through our thoughts, words, and actions. We must train ourselves to bring these elements of our lives in line with what God has instructed us to do in the Scriptures. Godly fear gives us the motivation to glorify God by acknowledging that without Him nothing we put our hands to will succeed. From the small, mindless things we engage in, like eating and drinking, to managing the difficulties of relationships and life- changing decisions, we must acknowledge God reverently as the One Who truly is in charge. The Bible clearly tells us to focus on things above (things that concern God).

God wants us to focus our minds, hearts and eyes on godly things, not on earthly things that cause us fear. We must go a step further when we discuss the fear of the Lord, because the Scripture also tells us that perfect love casts out all fear, and the beginning of wisdom is the fear of the Lord.

I was taught as a child that there is nothing scarier than God! Don't get me wrong; my parents didn't want me in a constant state of fear that our God was some boogie man waiting to pounce on me the moment I did something wrong!

They wanted me to know He loved me. They also wanted me to be wise enough to know that things happening in the world were temporary, but the promises of God are eternal.

On a personal level, God threatens our ego and our delusions about ourselves because He confronts us with truth and stands against the enemies of our freedom. Through this process, God destroys those things within us that the enemy can use against us so He can lift us up. William D. Eisenhower said, "Fear of the Lord is the beginning of wisdom, but love from the Lord is its completion."[3] If we walk in godly fear, nothing and no one can stand against the power of God working in our lives. Who is left for us to fear? No one!

Every time you are feeling fearful about stepping up to where God has called you, remember evil fear always comes from the enemy. It is a manifestation of his kingdom, which is darkness. This is the spirit that Satan uses to control people who love God, paralyzing them from living in the light and love of their Savior, Jesus Christ. However, if God truly is leading you in a certain direction, choose to trust Him. The time is now to face your fear, by confronting what has held you back and stymied your progress. Your desire to please God will be the fuel to help you overcome every fear. If you are in this type of struggle, let me encourage you to take Jesus' hand and go forward with His plan.

God never asks more of us than He has equipped us to handle. He has already empowered each of us to fulfill the task we have been assigned. Regardless of how great the task may be, the secret is not in trying harder to get it right or to get approval. It is in our demonstration of faith in God. He works everything out for our good! There is nothing Satan hates more than seeing God win our battles. Get your courage up! Make the enemy mad today and every day by claiming the strength of God and trusting Him more.

3 JoHanna Reardon, "*What Does It Mean To Fear God?*" 2013. Christianity Today.

Let Your Joy Be Full

God is an ever-present help in your time of need. You can ask Him for anything without fear or reservation. God does not love the martyrs of old more than He loves you. He fought for them, and He will do the same for you. The joy God offers to us is not like the joy we would experience if we won the lottery, received a promotion, or went on a dream vacation. These things would make anyone incredibly happy! But joy is something that only those who know God can experience despite their circumstances, failures, or hurt. It is the confidence in knowing that no matter what comes our way, He is with us. That makes everything alright.

A great illustration of the joy of the Lord can be seen in the life of King David. In the Book of Psalms, we read of David rejoicing even when he endured some of the most difficult situations of his life. There are many instances in Psalms that show us that the joy of the Lord is not only possible, but necessary for those who have accepted God's love and salvation. This type of joy goes against every humanistic feeling and emotion. It is not natural; it is supernatural.

Some people must work at accepting the joy of the Lord harder than others because they, as most of us, have practiced reacting to circumstances rather than relying on this great blessing to see us through. However, God has given us a daily supply of joy through His mercy. The God-type of joy is revealed through His great love for us – the sacrifice of His only Son. It is this same love that rescues us time and time again from the snare of the enemy.

Joy has the power to overcome fear. The Bible teaches that the joy of the Lord is our strength! We can overcome fear by allowing the joy of the Lord to fill every inch of our soul and spirit. When we take our concerns to God, we find fullness of joy in His presence, and out of the provision of His right hand, we can receive pleasures forevermore. (Psalm 16:11) To walk in the freedom He has designed for us, we must meet Him daily through prayer and praise to receive joy and pleasure, because His mercies are renewed every morning. (Lamentations 3:23) This is our place of hope; regardless of what's happening within the circle we stand; we can willfully walk away from the chaos into the intimacy of God knowing that our times are in His hands.

There is a distinct connection between fear and faith. We cannot overlook the number of people in Scripture who found divine strength in the most fearful times. Here are just a few: Daniel in the lion's den, Paul in the Philippian jail,

Moses standing before the Red Sea, and Peter and John on trial before the Sanhedrin. Each one looked death in the eye, and yet each found the faith to trust God and overcome fear. Our loving Savior has given us power to overcome fear as well.

Fear Not!

God does not beat around the bush with this command. He simply tells us *don't be afraid!* Yet, it is easy to see why many people believe they are living in a fear zone. Politicians, news media and our American culture play on our fears for their own personal benefit, but that doesn't mean the dangers are not real. Global terrorism, mass shootings, violent crimes, warfare spreading in unlikely places, epidemics of diseases, and natural disasters are all impacting us daily through media and technology.

These fearful events are often prevalent via entertainment and social media outlets and seep into our dreams, causing nightmares. The truth is most of the things we fear will never happen to us. But our anxieties and worries about them are very real. The Bible does not minimize the things we fear. The truth is, it warns us that the world will become more dangerous and frightening as the end times approach. So how do we obey God's command not to fear? This is what the Lord says:

- *"Fear   not, for I am with you; be not dismayed, for I am your God. I will strengthen you, yes, I will help you, I will uphold you with My righteous right hand."* (Isaiah 41:10, *NKJV*   )

- *"All your children shall be taught by the LORD, and great shall be the peace of your children. In righteousness you shall be established; you shall be far from oppression, for you shall not fear; and from terror, for it shall not come near you."* (Isaiah 54:13, 14, *NKJV*)

- *"Behold, I am the LORD, the God of all flesh. Is there anything too hard for Me?"* (Jeremiah 32:27, *NKJV*)

- • *"Are not two sparrows sold for a copper coin? And not one of them falls to the ground apart from your Father's will. But the very hairs of your head are all numbered. Do not fear; therefore, you are of more value than many sparrows. "* (Matthew 10:29-31, *NKJV*)

- • *"Fear not, little flock, for it is your Father's good pleasure to give you the kingdom. "* (Luke 12:32, *NKJV*)

- • *"Peace I leave with you, My peace I give to you; not as the world gives do, I give to you. Let not your heart be troubled, neither let it be afraid. "* (John 14:27, *NKJV*)

- • *"For He hath said, 'I will never leave thee nor forsake thee. So that we may boldly say, The Lord is my helper, and I will not fear what man shall do unto me. '"* (Hebrews 13:5, 6, *KJV*)

We can use these Scriptures to overcome the debilitating impact of fear. God invites us to cast all our cares on Him because He cares for us. We can ask Him for peace during our storms and He will answer. During your prayer time, remember, communication goes both ways. Don't just ask God for what you want and need and then say, "Amen." Allow Him to speak. Whether it is immediate, throughout the day or over the course of days, He will answer. Listen for His still, small voice.

The work of overcoming fear is accomplished by first differentiating between prudence, godly fear, and sinful fear. *Prudence* is defined as "wisdom, common sense or good judgment." It is not just the practice of wisdom by making wise choices, but it is also the art of avoiding evil. Practicing prudence will help you avoid choices that usher in fear. The Bible describes a prudent person as someone who is sensible and considers the consequences before taking the first step.

A prudent person also surrounds themselves with like-minded people who love knowledge and who avoid evil. This is unlike foolish people who naively proceed without caution and suffer the consequences of their bad choices. Foolish people also surround themselves with like-minded people who continuously talk about their issues and problems but lack the wisdom to make decisions to change their circumstances. Our goal should be to use prudence to live free of fear and avoid most trouble.

Hearing Tragic News and Walking by Faith

In 2008, my precious daughter was diagnosed with a rare form of breast cancer. Hearing the news sent fear through my entire body, even as the enemy worked against the corners of my mind. Everything around me seemed unsure, as I searched desperately for a foundation I could stand on. As you might imagine, it was a downright scary time! The news of her illness stabbed my heart like a two-edge sword, cutting deeply to my very core.

I remember her phone call like it was yesterday: "Mom," she said with more desperation than I had ever heard in her voice before. Hearing the emotion, I demanded to know what was wrong as she struggled to find the words to tell me about the pending darkness which would soon completely overwhelm us. I remember the long pregnant pause she took before explaining how the doctors had come to their conclusion. I felt fear for her and within her as our two-year journey for her physical healing began.

After reality set in, I realized that together we had to fight against this killer called cancer. First, I prayed and asked God to forgive my worry and unbelief. I had to declare, through tear- stained eyes, my confession of faith concerning His will for my daughter's life. After some time, I felt a peace that surpassed my understanding, subdued my logic, and left me helpless in the face of earthly facts. Even as I watched the gift of physical life leave my daughter, and the presence of eternal life invade her room, I knew that my family and I were accompanied with the presence of God's perfect love. He gently overshadowed me with an unreasonable peace that ruled my broken heart.

God commands us to fear not, yet sinful fear has a way of making it seem impossible. This type of fear attempts to pull us away from our biblical foundation. The easiest way to determine if fear is sinful or godly is by questioning whether the way we are acting will bring glory to God or not. That includes what we do as well as what we refuse to do! When we get caught up in sinful fear, it usually results from our desire for the approval of others or our desire to control the situation instead of relying on God and His Word.

Godly fear shows up when we trust God so much that we no longer allow ourselves to interfere with or question His plan. This type of fear wrestles down thoughts of inadequacy and chases worry and anxiety away because our confidence is in God and not ourselves. The reality is the price for our sins and shortcomings was covered by the blood Jesus shed for us on Calvary. Because God's love is enough, we don't have to worry. The peace we find in Him brings us to worship instead of worry, and to faith instead of fear. This is the place God is calling us to.

When fear grips your very being, take the necessary steps to overthrow it immediately. First, pray about it. Make your requests known to God by going boldly before His throne. Realize that you are the daughter or son of God. Two, cultivate right-thinking by disciplining your mind with positive thoughts. This will prevent you from falling prey to the tricks of the devil. Three, meditate on God's Word and regain your stance of faith. Then manage your reactions and responses. This step will usher you into the peace that only God can provide.

If your life now or in times past has been plagued by fear, it is time that you face it once and for all. Stand up and give fear an eviction notice. Put it out of your heart and mind and begin to live victoriously in the power of God and His love everlasting!

CHAPTER ELEVEN

From Denim to Diamonds: Unconquerable and Indestructible

According to the *Oxford Dictionary*, the definition of a *jewel* is "A precious stone, typically a single crystal or a cut, or a polished piece of a lustrous or translucent mineral." One of the most precious stones known to man is the diamond. The Greek word for diamond is *adamas* which means "unconquerable and indestructible." In 327 BC, Alexander the Great brought the first diamond to Europe from India, the land where diamonds were first discovered. Romans believed that diamonds had power to ward off evil spirits and wore them as talismans. In 1477, Mary of Burgundy received a diamond engagement ring from Archduke Maximilian of Austria. As a result, the history and tradition of the diamond engagement ring continues to this day.

The largest diamond, the Cullinan, was discovered in 1905 and weighed in at 3,106 carats. It was named after Thomas Cullinan, owner of the Premier Mine in South Africa. Its nickname is the Great Star of Africa. The Crater of Diamonds State Park in Arkansas is the world's only diamond mine open to the public where one can experience a dig-free operation for tourists and rock enthusiasts. A diamond nicknamed "Uncle Sam" was found there in 1924. The diamond is the hardest of all gemstones known to man.

It is also the simplest in composition and is made up of only one element—common carbon. Approximately 250 tons of ore must be mined and processed from the average Kimberlite pipe to produce a one-carat polished diamond of gem quality. Kimberlite is the name given to volcanic rock.

Diamonds are carried to the earth's surface by volcanic eruptions; very few diamonds survive the hazardous journey from the depths of the earth to its surface. Diamonds are brittle; if hit hard with a hammer, a diamond will shatter or splinter. Even though a diamond can be broken, a diamond seemingly lasts forever.

In contrast, denim is worn as casual clothing. The value of denim does not compare to that of a diamond. For this discussion, denim represents the basics of who we are, or the struggles of trying to become who God has called us to be.

It's a heavy material, like many of the things in our lives that weigh us down. Diamonds, on the other hand, represent who we become as we go through the trials and tribulations in our lives. The trials and tribulations can be likened to violent, hot, and disruptive volcanic activity that produces the rarest stones, known as diamonds.

Although you started this journey as a diamond in the rough, your value was not readily apparent. You may have been overlooked and picked over. It took time for the dirt and rough edges to wear off, but God spoke over your life and called you a diamond when others only considered you insignificant. What other people did not know was that diamonds that have been cut, polished, and touched by too many hands lose their value. God held you and kept you for a time such as this! It has always been His plan to bring you from the background into the forefront. People will look at you and wonder why you were chosen and why you matter! They will only see your flaws and the dirt from the mountains you survived.

Many of your flaws were formed from the pressures of the mountains you endured. You thought you needed to be shiny for your brilliance to matter. But the truth is, a rough diamond is the purest and most natural form of diamond there is because it has not yet been polished or perfected. God has chosen you for your uniqueness, your special qualities, and your flaws, which add value and strength to who you are.

Be careful not to blend in with the crowd. They chase what's in fashion, which causes a fluctuation in value. Rough diamonds have the advantage of never

"going out of style." God never intended for you to tailor yourself after others. His Word tells us not to conform to this world, but to be transformed by the renewing of our minds. This implies changing your thought patterns from confirmative to transformational. *"And do not be fashioned according to this age but be transformed by the renewing of the mind that you may prove what the will of God is, that which is good and well pleasing and perfect."* (Romans 12:2)

In the original Greek language of the New Testament, the word used for *transformation* is *metamorphosis.* The biological definition for metamorphosis, according to *www.dictionary.com* , is "a profound change in form from one stage to the next in the life history of an organism, as from the caterpillar to the pupa and from the pupa to the adult butterfly." Although an outward change in appearance takes place, the change comes from within the life of the organism. A caterpillar is born to become a

184

butterfly, just as you were born again to become a refined diamond. The caterpillar doesn't put on a butterfly costume or strive to act like a butterfly. The nutrients it consumes and assimilates causes it to become a real, genuine butterfly.

A caterpillar's transformation into a butterfly is an excellent example of what the Bible speaks of concerning the believer's transformation into the image of Christ. Finding our place in Him is what matters above everything. Transformation takes time, and as children of the Most-High God, we must consume the Word to nourish our spirit. This process causes our spiritual metabolism to grow, as we continue to develop into valuable life-long diamonds in Him!

The following list was taken from the Bibles for America web site. It states that calling on the name of Jesus throughout the day and telling Him how much we love Him facilitates our transformation. The Word of God is our daily bread. In addition:

- We should sing with our spirit to the Lord.
- We should pray with our spirit.
- We should pray over what we read in the Bible.
- We should give thanks to God.
- We should praise God.
- We should preach the Gospel or speak about Christ to others.

Becoming a Diamond Queen

Although you may have endured great pressure, contradiction and misinformation during your life, it's time for you to get rid of the mental mirror that reminds you of things that have hindered you in the past. Give the queen in you permission to outshine your past. It doesn't matter what your size, shape, color, or circumstances may be. You were created to be not only a queen, but a *diamond queen*. A queen is a woman who has a royal place, but a diamond queen creates her place based on her ability to overcome issues that would have taken a lesser woman out. Her sparkle shines through the hardest dirt. Start telling yourself the truth today! Say this out loud right now: "I am perfect for my purpose. I was fearfully, carefully, skillfully and wonderfully created."

If anyone calls on you because of your remarkable talent or skill, answer the call! There is no better person to fulfil the request than you! You are truly a remarkable woman, and its high time you acknowledge that fact. Diamonds in the raw hold great value, but they are difficult to recognize by the untrained eye. It is nearly impossible to mount an uncut diamond. However, you were created to be mounted, crowned, and put on display because you are a *diamond queen* .

186

You may have thought you lost something because of the circumstances you have faced, but the cuts of life are bringing forth great brilliance in you. Don't be mistaken: your cuts are not blemishes. They have come to make you strong. Cuts allow rays of light to flow through the many facets of your life, displaying your beauty. All of us are at different stages in our lives. For example, I may have endured a simple cut, which forms its own beauty. On the other hand, you may have a multifaceted cut, which allows a greater amount of light to flow through.

Each cut was handled by the Skilled Jeweler, who knows the intended outcome. However, appreciation of who you are must begin within you. This level of appreciation-shift begins with renewing your mind and once and for all resolving the conflict over who you are and what your talent and purpose is in life. Let's review a few points to help you settle into your kingdom, dear queen

- **Practice Mindfulness** - the practice of maintaining a nonjudgmental state of heightened or complete awareness of one's thoughts, emotions, or experiences on a moment-to-moment basis. (*Merriam-Webster.com*) To practice this art, there are components we must include in our practice. Being mindful means making peace with who you are and coming to grips with what is most important to you. Don't worry; take a deep breath and dive in headfirst. You will receive great satisfaction from bringing this practice into your daily routine.

- **Awareness** – To begin this practice, pay attention to you, and only you.

This means you must establish time in each day to simply be quiet. Whether that is 5, 10, 15 minutes or more, make that time for yourself to assess where you are in the day and address what you are feeling and experiencing in present tense. Turn off the phone, TV, music, and anything else that demands your attention and pulls your mind away from you. If you have family – children, spouse, others – communicate your need to have this time and take it without guilt. Quietly notice your thoughts, feelings, and physical sensations as they happen. Your goal isn't to clear your mind or to stop thinking. It is to become more aware of your thoughts and feelings. This awareness does not mean getting lost in thoughts or emotions. It means hearing them, feeling them, and recognizing them as your own.

- **Acceptance** – This may be difficult for those who have dealt with criticism and those who may be uncomfortable with their own thoughts and feelings. I am asking you to dismiss any old, outdated thoughts that may have hindered you or tried to shame you in some way in the past.

Begin acknowledging your feelings, thoughts, and sensations in a nonjudgmental manner. As you notice thoughts, feelings, or sensations, acknowledge them as yours. For example, if you are feeling nervous, just say to yourself, "I notice I am feeling nervous." Don't feel pressure to change the feeling or thought. Just acknowledge that it is there. The Bible teaches us that God is mindful of us, and He notices everything we do. The Scriptures tell us that not even a small bird can fall to the ground without God knowing.

There is no one who cares more about you than God does. He is fully aware of whatever concerns you, worries you, causes you fear or keeps you up at night. He knows you well and best. God cares for you and He is perfecting everything that concerns you. Because God is alert and focused on you, you should be alert and focused on your thoughts as well.

Mindfulness will help guide you to your purpose and provide direction for your destiny. To practice this art form, consider mindful meditation and mindful walking.

Mindful Meditation

- **Meditation**: the revolving around and around in the mind of something of great importance; turning a subject over and over until one is talking or murmuring to oneself about it; to utter, imagine, pray, speak *(Merriam-Webster.com)*.

- **Ponder**: to weigh something in the mind until all barriers that stand in the way of understanding it fully have been removed; is used to describe the rolling or flattening of bumpy ground to make it into a roadway *(Merriam-Webster.com)*.

- **Consider**: to see, understand by looking long at a problem; to return again and again to the subject; to note carefully, to fully observe, to behold, and, in beholding, discover *(Merriam-Webster.com)*.

We must learn to think what our hearts already know, for it is our thoughts that produce our lifestyles. What we are in our thoughts today will determine the way we live tomorrow. The Bible teaches us to renew our minds by transforming our thoughts by reading and meditating on God's Word. We can only do that by studying God's Word and believing in our heart what we read.

As you practice mindfulness, you will learn more about yourself. You're probably thinking, *"I already know myself."* Most people feel that way, but this practice helps us to identify more clearly who we are. You must believe in the good in your heart, which God has placed inside you. Begin by sitting in a comfortable place, hearing and feeling your breathing. Notice the physical sensation of air filling your lungs, and the release of air out of your nostrils. When your mind wanders, and it will, simply pay attention to your thoughts at that moment and return to your breathing. Do this for several minutes until you feel a sense of calm and awareness of the rhythm of your breathing. Read or recite Scriptures or words of affirmation in your mind that encourage and uplift your soul.

Mindful Walking

A queen must always be aware of her steps to ensure that they are ordered by the Lord. Being mindful while walking means to become very aware of your walk. Notice how your body moves and feels with each step you take. This will tell you where your stressors are and if your steps are even and rhythmic. Then take in your surroundings; use your senses to speak to your mind. What do you see? Colors? Shapes? Textures? What do you hear? Birds? Dogs? Wind? What do you smell? Flowers? Grass? Trees? What do you feel? Heat? Free? Love? Anxiety?

As you become mindful of yourself and your surroundings, begin to put a demand on your walk. Bring peace in your steps, love in every breath, and wholeness as you move toward your desired direction. Practice this level of mindfulness until it becomes part of your daily routine. When things enter a queen's atmosphere, trying to create drama, problems, or issues, she exercises her God- given authority to change her atmosphere and watch things move on her behalf.

God has prepared for us abundant life, and this life must be lived moment by moment, while being keenly aware of our surroundings. Determine to experience everything God has for you more deeply by experiencing it through your senses first – seeing, feeling, hearing, tasting and smelling. Then experience it in your spirit through the power of the Holy Spirit, through the love of God, and with a sound mind. These gateways produce within you the fullness of the abundant life God has in mind for you and will empower you to minister to others, loving them as you love yourself.

Only out of the abundance of love that you have for yourself can you express agape love toward others. When you finally embrace you and the queen within you, without condemnation and judgment, you will begin to freely express the beautiful light God designed you to be. You are on the road to walking in your destiny of peace, love and harmony, just as God intended.

Many women are totally unaware of themselves, their surroundings, and their true power. If you are one them, and you have been living life as it comes – without expectation and without putting a demand on your day – you are not living like the queen you were designed to be. Don't allow abundant life to pass you by! You must seize this moment to ascertain the depth of your royalty. To seize the moment, you must push harder and reach further than you ever have before. You must take the blinders off and see your victories as gifts from God and your failures as preparation for greater things. No failure, guilt or problems can stop you when you are mindful of what's happening in your life.

Practice giving God all the glory through meditation. Thank Him in advance of your victories. This simple act will command a multitude of blessings to pour into your life. The Bible says God will keep your mind in perfect peace if you are mindful of Him. Only the natural will reduce symptoms of depression, stress and anxiety and improve your memory and ability to focus. It will also improve your ability to adapt and manage emotions, especially in stressful situations. Meditation accompanied by praise will also make you keenly aware that God is in everything, transcending time, and generations, everywhere, always. This awareness changes how you see everything, pushing you to make that extra step, knowing you're almost at your goal. Finishing any way other than strong is unacceptable.

Conclusion

This book is a call to action that begins in your spirit. It is a small flame that should ignite a fire that will burn through every fiber of your being! You not only matter to me, more importantly, you matter to God. Let this assurance empower you to move to the next level of abundant life.

The truths you have uncovered in these pages, will help you take inventory of your life. Further, it will give you the power to scrutinize anything and anybody who is not striving for greater, reaching for more and seeking God's highest. There will be those who will attempt to discourage you. Expect it! Perhaps the hardest thing to overcome will be the discouragement you will receive from those you love, trust and admire.

It is at that time that you must refuse to give up. When these moments come – and they will – take time to remember why you decided to pursue your dream in the first place. When you find that place, reprint it in your mind, hold it in your heart, and rekindle it in your spirit. It is in these difficult situations that mindfulness works best. Remain confident and stay connected to the truths found in God's Word. This will revive your dream and cause it to breathe again.

Now that you realize how much you matter to God; it should become easier to let go the opinions others have of you. It may take time for this to become actualized in your spirit but keep at it. It is the negative thoughts, ideas and dreams of our past that attempt to hold power over us when we allow them. However, when the truth is embraced, you can successfully do as Paul did: forget those things which are behind and press toward the mark of a higher calling. This, my dear sister and queen, is freedom!

Your freedom in Christ is neither a pipe dream nor a daydream; this reality has rested on many queens before you. The dream God has given you is bigger than what you have imagined. It is a God- sized dream that should replace all the failed dreams your mind has rehearsed over time. Protect it with all your heart and don't allow fear to paralyze your efforts. If your steps are ordered by the Lord, He will see you through. Lean and depend on Him because through Him,

you can do *all* things!

The act of renewing your mind to receive what God originally intended for your life will energize your resolve in everything you set your mind to do. This seed of truth gives endless possibilities to a life without walls or barriers, a life free from the bondage of this world and the people who are bound by it. You will be free to express your God-given talents and abilities whenever and wherever He leads.

As a diamond queen, you have been called and anointed by God. Walk in this power; it will restore your self-worth and accelerate your purpose! It also allows God to breathe into you the grace to be the mom you want to be, the entrepreneur you're working to be, and the leader you were born to be. Don't fall into the trap of comparing yourself to others. Your outcome may seem the same as others, but your path is unique to you, your desires, and experiences. Never try to make your life peg fit into someone else's life hole. It will not fit.

Great women seek great counsel! They seek other women with proven records of trial, error and, most importantly, success. As you travel this transforming journey, seek those who will walk with you and fight for you. You do not need anyone in your inner circle who will help you make excuses or pull you into a downward spiral along with them.

The people in your inner circle must be for you! This is the qualification required of friends, lovers, and others. If they fail this test, they should not be in your closest circle. Removing the dead weight found in some relationships, will set your spirit free. You may find it difficult to let some people go, because they feed your old self, but with the newness of your mind and the freedom of your spirit, you will soar to heights you could never reach with them. Let them go!

Today, you are stronger than you were before you started, so stay on the mountain peak, never settling for the ground. You are an eagle; you were made to love the leap and experience the thrill of soaring on strong wings. Although you may have endured the limitations of your thoughts or the negative words and abusive actions of others, by reading this book, you have learned to hate the confinement of the yard. Therefore, never lose your inbred heritage of soaring by lowering your standards.

No matter what you've gone through, *you matter!* No matter how hard it may seem, *you matter!* Even if you are in a struggle right now, it does not negate the fact that *you matter!* Claim it today. Shout it from the mountaintop! Make it your response to everyone who attempts to contradict you: *"Yes, I do matter!"*

198

www.ingramcontent.com/pod-product-compliance
Lightning Source LLC
Chambersburg PA
CBHW051827090426
42736CB00011B/1686